THE AGE OF GOD-KINGS

TimeFrame 3000-1500 BC

CRETE AND THE AEGEAN

EGYPT

Time Frame: 3000-1500 BC

THE INDUS VALLEY AND CHINA

MESOPOTAMIA

Other Publications:
THE TIME-LIFE GARDENER'S GUIDE
MYSTERIES OF THE UNKNOWN
FIX IT YOURSELF
FITNESS, HEALTH & NUTRITION
SUCCESSFUL PARENTING
HEALTHY HOME COOKING
UNDERSTANDING COMPUTERS
LIBRARY OF NATIONS
THE ENCHANTED WORLD
THE KODAK LIBRARY OF CREATIVE PHOTOGRAPHY
GREAT MEALS IN MINUTES
THE CIVIL WAR
PLANET EARTH
COLLECTOR'S LIBRARY OF THE CIVIL WAR
THE EPIC OF FLIGHT
THE GOOD COOK
WORLD WAR II
HOME REPAIR AND IMPROVEMENT
THE OLD WEST

For information on and a full description of
any of the Time-Life Books series listed above,
please call 1-800-621-7026 or write:
Reader Information
Time-Life Customer Service
P.O. Box C-32068
Richmond, Virginia 23261-2068

This volume is one in a series that tells the story
of humankind.

THE AGE OF GOD-KINGS

TimeFrame 3000-1500 BC

BY THE EDITORS OF TIME-LIFE BOOKS

TIME-LIFE BOOKS, ALEXANDRIA, VIRGINIA

Time-Life Books Inc.
is a wholly owned subsidiary of
TIME INCORPORATED

FOUNDER: Henry R. Luce 1898-1967

Editor-in-Chief: Henry Anatole Grunwald
Chairman and Chief Executive Officer:
J. Richard Munro
President and Chief Operating Officer:
N. J. Nicholas Jr.
Chairman of the Executive Committee:
Ralph P. Davidson
Corporate Editor: Ray Cave
Executive Vice President, Books:
Kelso F. Sutton
Vice President, Books: George Artandi

TIME-LIFE BOOKS INC.

EDITOR: George Constable
Executive Editor: Ellen Phillips
Director of Design: Louis Klein
Director of Editorial Resources:
Phyllis K. Wise
Editorial Board: Russell B. Adams Jr., Dale
M. Brown, Roberta Conlan, Thomas H.
Flaherty, Lee Hassig, Donia Ann Steele,
Rosalind Stubenberg, Kit van Tulleken,
Henry Woodhead
Director of Photography and Research:
John Conrad Weiser

PRESIDENT: Christopher T. Linen
Chief Operating Officer: John M. Fahey Jr.
Senior Vice Presidents: James L. Mercer,
Leopoldo Toralballa
Vice Presidents: Stephen L. Bair, Ralph
J. Cuomo, Neal Goff, Stephen L. Gold-
stein, Juanita T. James, Hallett Johnson III,
Carol Kaplan, Susan J. Maruyama, Robert
H. Smith, Paul R. Stewart, Joseph J. Ward
Director of Production Services:
Robert J. Passantino

Editorial Operations
Copy Chief: Diane Ullius
Editorial Operations Manager:
Caroline A. Boubin
Production: Celia Beattie
Quality Control: James J. Cox (director)
Library: Louise D. Forstall

Correspondents: Elisabeth Kraemer-Singh
(Bonn); Maria Vincenza Aloisi (Paris); Ann
Natanson (Rome). Valuable assistance
was also provided by: Mirka Gondicas
(Athens); Caroline Alcock, Christine
Hinze, Caroline Lucas, Linda Proud (Lon-
don); Liz Brown, Christina Lieberman
(New York); Ann Wise (Rome); Dick Berry
(Tokyo); Traudl Lessing (Vienna).

TIME FRAME

SERIES DIRECTOR: Henry Woodhead
Designer: Dale Pollekoff
Series Administrator:
Philip Brandt George

Editorial Staff for *The Age of God-Kings*
Associate Editor: Robin Richman
(pictures)
Text Editors: Stephen G. Hyslop, Ray
Jones, David S. Thomson
Researchers: Karin Kinney (text); Patti H.
Cass, Patricia McKinney (pictures)
Assistant Designers: Elissa E. Baldwin,
Paul Graboff, Alan Pitts
Copy Coordinators: Vivian Noble, Jayne
E. Rohrich
Picture Coordinator: Renée DeSandies
Editorial Assistant: Patricia D. Whiteford

Special Contributors: Ronald H. Bailey,
Champ Clark, George G. Daniels, Donald
Dale Jackson, Bryce Walker (text); Holly
Idelson, Robbie D. Steel (research)

CONSULTANTS

General
JOHN R. McNEILL, Assistant Professor,
Department of History, Georgetown Uni-
versity, Washington, D.C.

Egypt
CHRISTOPHE BARBOTIN, Conservateur
du Département des Antiquités Égyptiennes, Musée du Louvre, Paris

ROBERT S. BIANCHI, Assistant Curator,
Department of Egyptian, Classical and An-
cient Middle Eastern Art, The Brooklyn
Museum, Brooklyn

MARK LEHRNER, Director, Giza Plateau
Mapping Project, Yale University, New
Haven, Connecticut; member, The Ameri-
can Research Center, Egypt

DAVID O'CONNOR, Associate Curator,
Egyptian Section, The University Museum,
University of Pennsylvania, Philadelphia

Mesopotamia
T. C. MITCHELL, Keeper of Western Asiatic Antiquities, British Museum, London

RICHARD L. ZETTLER, Assistant Professor, Department of Anthropology, and Assistant Curator, Near Eastern Section, The
University Museum, University of Pennsylvania, Philadelphia

Indus Valley
MICHAEL JANSEN, Director, The
Mohenjo-Daro Research Project, Aachen
University, Aachen, Federal Republic of
Germany

Southeast Asia
JOYCE C. WHITE, Visiting Assistant Cura-
tor/Lecturer, The University Museum,
University of Pennsylvania, Philadelphia

Crete
W. JOSEPH SHAW, Professor of Fine Arts,
University of Toronto, Toronto

**Library of Congress Cataloging in Publication
Data**

The Age of god-kings.
  Bibliography: p.
  Includes index.
  1. History, Ancient.   I. Time-Life Books.
D57.A34 1987   930   87-10229
ISBN 0-8094-6400-4
ISBN 0-8094-6401-2 (lib. bdg.)

CONTENTS

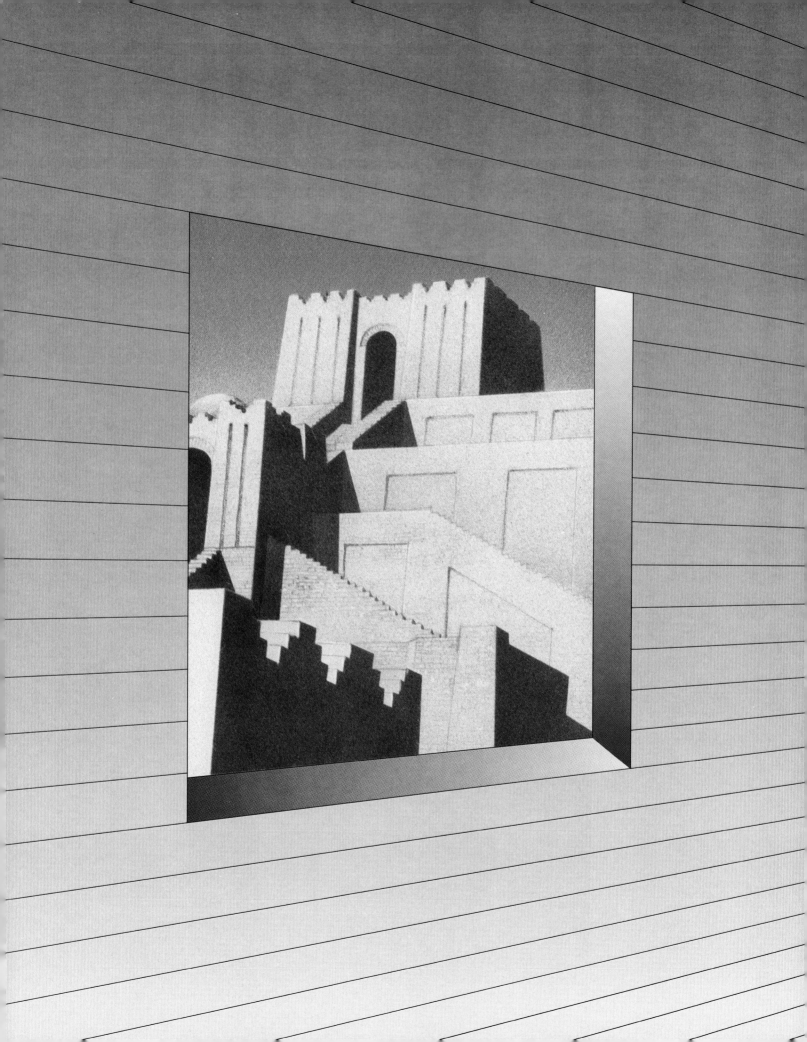

BREAKTHROUGH AT SUMER

The Middle Eastern sun burned down out of a cloudless sky, baking the earth and shriveling the few plants that had sprouted after the sparse spring rains. A hot wind from the desert to the southwest stirred dust devils that scoured the featureless plain. No hills rose on the horizon; there was scarcely a tree to offer relief from the shimmering heat. Only two sluggish rivers broke the monotony of the landscape as they flowed southward, a pair of brown ribbons in a brown void.

The water attracted some life. Birds darted over the marshes where the rivers had overrun their banks; schools of fish ruffled the shallows. There were also a few humans — people living in mud huts on the edges of the marshes where the soil was moist. Scratching in the earth, they cultivated meager plots and they kept a few cows and pigs, which grazed in the wetlands. But for the most part, the plain lay somnolent in the implacable glare.

This was the valley formed by the Tigris and the Euphrates rivers as it existed 9,000 years ago — or about the year 7000 BC, based on the modern calendar. Situated deep in the Middle East, more than 600 miles east of the Mediterranean, the region seemed an unredeemable wasteland. Yet by 3000 BC, an astonishingly different panorama was unfolding. Along the length of the valley, magnificent cities sprawled on the riverbanks. Around them, fields of grain spread like a tide of fecundity across the once-desolate flatlands. Groves of date palms swayed in the wind, offering fruit and shade. Within the massive walls that ringed the cities, temples towered over both streetscape and plain. There were brick palaces and mansions, and street after street of comfortable houses. People thronged the avenues and marketplaces; in hundreds of workshops, artisans turned out all manner of goods, from pottery to sparkling jewelry. On holy days, processions of the worshipful wound through the streets to the temples.

What had happened in this land that the Greeks later called Mesopotamia, meaning "between the rivers," was the most crucial event in human history: the birth of civilization. The descendants of those Stone Age farmers clinging to the edges of the swamps — a people who came to be known as the Sumerians and their land, Sumer — had turned the apparent inadequacies of their homeland to immense, world-changing advantage.

At the time of the Sumerians' rise, the majority of the planet's population were living as nomads; they roamed in small bands, providing food for themselves by hunting animals and by gathering the seeds and stalks of wild plants. On the broad savannahs of Africa, in the forested wildernesses of Europe, and in Australia and the Americas, human beings clothed themselves in the skins of animals and sought shelter in caves or crude lean-tos. They remained close to the wild herds throughout the animals' seasonal migrations and devoted their waking hours to sheer survival. Some peoples had advanced well beyond their hunting-and-gathering past, however. The first to break out of the primordial pattern — a strategy for survival that had been followed ever since the human species came into being hundreds of thousands of years earlier — were some inhabitants of the Middle East. Over thousands of years, they learned to domesticate sheep and goats and to cultivate crops of wheat and barley. Now they could stop roaming and settle in one place. These people, the first farmers, established their agricultural villages as early as 8500 BC to the north and east of Mesopotamia, in hilly regions where rain was plentiful. The practice of agriculture spread rapidly, and soon farmers devised irrigation techniques that allowed them to grow crops without the benefit of rainfall.

Irrigated crops sustained sizable settlements well before the first Sumerian cities appeared on the Mesopotamian plain. The biblical city of Jericho, a center for salt trade, flourished during the seventh millennium BC in the desert near the north end of the Dead Sea. Water diverted from a spring nourished its fields. Similarly, 500 miles to the north in Asia Minor, irrigated crops fed the people of Çatal Hüyük, a settlement that sprang up about 6500 BC near a field of obsidian, a dark volcanic glass valued for making mirrors, jewelry, and knives. Although both Jericho and Çatal Hüyük achieved populations of several thousand people, their future was constrained, since they depended for their existence on a single prized commodity and lacked agricultural resources that would enable them to expand further.

The Sumerians, with access to two rivers, were the ones to develop irrigated agriculture on a truly grand scale. Tapping the waters of their rivers — primarily the Euphrates — they cultivated vast stretches of alluvial desert and brought them into production. The result was a surplus of grain far beyond the day-to-day needs of the farmers tending the fields — a surplus that gave the people of Sumer the time to develop new skills and new ways of making do. They became inventive and thoughtful. Artisans, traders, priests, scribes, and merchants came into being, sustained by the efforts of the farmers. A system of government emerged, as well as an organized religion and a new order of social classes — all the elements of what would one day be recognized as a civilization.

In time, the Sumerians forged city-states and then a nation. Sumer's kings established theories of justice, raised armies, and built networks of trade. Most important, the Sumerians invented the first form of writing, so that one generation could pass knowledge down to another in a permanent form. Sumerian scribes began recounting the deeds of their kings — that is, they initiated recorded history. They were the first to write down epic poems and meditations on the meaning of life.

Within 300 years of the emergence of Sumerian culture in its full glory, the seeds of civilization took root along the banks of some of the world's other great rivers: the Nile of Egypt, the Indus of modern-day Pakistan, and the Yellow River of China. Brilliant flowerings would occur at all of these places, but Sumer had been the first. It had launched humanity on a strange and wonderful adventure, and its accomplishments would be printed indelibly in the human consciousness. The remarkable interaction between the Sumerians' fertile minds and their unpromising but ultimately fruitful land gave birth to ways of thinking and acting that can be detected in the thoughts and customs of people to this day.

The questions of who the first Sumerians were, where they came from, and when they arrived in the Tigris-Euphrates Valley remain unanswered. A dark-haired and light-skinned people, they probably originated in a region to the east or northeast of Mesopotamia; their language was related to one spoken near the Caspian Sea. It is likely that they arrived in the valley around 8500 BC, when the first primitive agricultural villages were being established there. In any case, the first Sumerians clustered in the far south of the valley, on the borders of the reed-choked swamps that covered much of the delta where the Tigris and Euphrates flowed into the Persian Gulf.

The early settlers soon discovered that winter rains caused the surrounding desert to bloom luxuriantly before again being baked rock-hard by the summer sun. The soil along the banks of the rivers was some of the most fertile on earth, deep and rich in minerals washed down from the mountains where the Tigris and Euphrates had their headwaters. In this alluvium, blessedly free of stones and stumps that plagued farmers elsewhere, barley and wheat and vegetables would grow easily. Furthermore, the soil was frequently enriched by a fresh layer of silt left by spring floods; it could be farmed year after year, generation after generation. The trick was to keep the seedlings thriving through Mesopotamia's torrid and rainless summers.

The Sumerians' first attempts to irrigate their fields were modest; they simply carried vessels of water from the rivers to their small plots. Later the farmers made narrow breaches in the natural levees that had built up over the centuries along the riverbanks,

Sumer, the world's first civilization, flourished about 3500 BC along the banks of the lower Tigris and Euphrates rivers in the heart of the Middle East. Diverting the rivers' waters to irrigate fields of grain, the Sumerians amassed agricultural wealth and used it to nurture such powerful city-states as Uruk, Ur, and Lagash. Soon these cities were engaged in trade with many other parts of the ancient world — with mountain tribes to the north and east, and with peoples on the Mediterranean coast to the west. Along the trade routes traveled not only the produce of Sumer's fields and the products of its workshops but also word of Sumer's greatest cultural achievement, the invention of writing. In time, Sumer's influence reached Egypt, Asia Minor, and beyond.

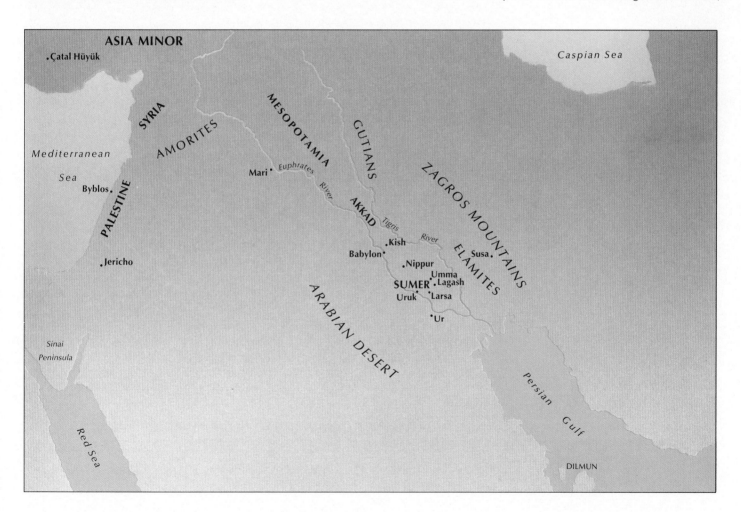

diverting some of the flow. They also created small mud dams, allowing the water to collect in basins. From these it could be dipped into shallow irrigation ditches with the *shaduf,* a bailing bucket mounted on a long counterweighted pole. Soon these ditches laced the fields near the rivers; in time, gangs of workers excavated long canals to channel water to fields several miles from the rivers.

As their fields moved away from the soft muck of the levees to harder ground, the Sumerians invented that rudimentary but all-important agricultural tool, the plow. Before, farmers poked holes in the ground for seed, using pointed sticks or animal horns. The Sumerians' first plow was nothing more than a crooked tree branch; one person would pull it while another pushed, forcing the crooked end into the soil and thus creating a furrow. Then, in the course of the fourth millennium, farmers contrived a copper plow and harnessed their oxen to it, thereby uniting what previously had been two separate vocations, dirt farming and animal husbandry. By about 3000 BC, they were using a tougher implement made of bronze, an alloy of copper and tin, which made it possible for the Sumerians to cultivate far larger plots.

As the agricultural effort expanded, the construction of networks of canals and dikes required the combined efforts of numer-ous workers and demanded unprecedent-ed cooperation from the entire community. Before Sumer existed, the traditional unit of labor among nomadic herders and primi-tive farmers alike had been the family or clan. But families or clans working sepa-rately were incapable of digging and main-taining complex irrigation systems. People were forced to band together and, while not forgetting ties of kinship, to recog-nize that they owed a larger loyalty to village, town, and eventually city. The col-lecting of people in ever-larger communi-ties produced in Sumer — as it would in other societies — the interaction and innovation that engendered civilized life.

At the same time, the scale of their irrigation projects helped push the Sumerians toward specialization — the division of labor that has been a mark of all civilizations. Sumer's fields produced such bountiful harvests that not everyone had to farm. Manag-ers, or planners, emerged, men who laid out the canals and dikes and made sure the flow of water reached its destination. These specialists developed a new technology: instruments for measuring, surveying, and calculating slopes and flow patterns, and the mathematics that would make those measurements useful. The early managers probably also helped devise the new plow made with metals brought from ore-rich mountain areas. All metals had to be obtained by trade in distant regions; the deep, fertile loam of the Tigris-Euphrates plain contained no deposits whatever of ores that would yield copper, tin, or iron.

Their revolutionary agriculture also encouraged the Sumerians to pursue the sci-ence of astronomy, observing and correlating movements of the sun and moon to establish a reliable calendar. The one they came up with, based on lunar months of twenty-eight days, quite accurately predicted the onset of the seasons and reminded farmers when to plant and harvest their crops.

Specialists probably also deserve credit for another of Sumer's great technological achievements — the invention of the wheel. It seems likely that wheels were first employed in pottery making. Artisans would throw a lump of clay on a horizontal plate balanced on an axle, then spin this to shape a round utensil — as potters would do from that time on. The Sumerians were the first to think of flipping the potter's wheel on its side and adapting it for locomotion. The wheel enabled farmers to work land that was at a considerable distance from their village or town. An ox or a donkey hitched to a wheeled cart could pull three times the load the animal could carry on its back or drag on a flat-bottomed sledge.

While some specialists spurred the advance of farming, others focused on spiritual matters. An increasingly numerous priesthood elaborated a complete cosmological system that explained all aspects of the natural and human world. The Sumerian religion proved to be so powerful that it endured for 3,000 years, greatly influencing the succession of peoples who occupied Mesopotamia after Sumer's decline.

Part of the religion's strength lay in its rich diversity of gods. The Sumerian pantheon contained no fewer than 3,000 deities. Virtually every realm of nature and human endeavor was presided over by a different god or goddess. Rain, sun, moon, vegetation — each had its own deity. So did more prosaic things such as plows, picks, and molds for making bricks. In addition, each settlement had its own particular god to whom, the priests averred, it had been assigned on the day of the world's birth.

Advances in the design of the plow boosted the productivity of the Sumerian peasant. By 3000 BC, the original wooden plowshare, barely strong enough to scratch the ground without bending, had given way in Sumer to a much sturdier bronze blade; some plows were equipped with funnels that deposited seed as soon as the ground was broken. Such tools proved so efficient that a tenant farmer who paid as much as one-half his annual yield in rent might still have food left to support his family.

The gods were not considered equal. Chief among them was a quartet that controlled what the Sumerians believed were the four main spheres of nature: heaven, air, earth, and water. And of these four deities, one always reigned supreme. At first, the most powerful of the gods was An, ruler of the heavens. Later he was superseded by Enlil, god of the air.

All of the Sumerian gods, both major and minor, were endowed with the emotions and physical needs of humankind. The Sumerian deities ate, drank, loved, married, and fought among themselves. They also communicated their wishes to the human race, letting the priests and priestesses know what they wanted through such omens as the shape of a liver found in a sacrificial sheep.

It was not a particularly hopeful religion. According to one Sumerian myth, people had been molded out of clay by the gods for the sole purpose of serving as their slaves. Failure to revere and propitiate the deities could bring catastrophe: floods, drought, pestilence, or raids by tribes from the hills. Such calamities frequently did afflict the Sumerians, and apprehension generated in the people of the plain a chronic anxiety. This made religion powerful and pervasive — and greatly benefited the priests and their temples. Generous offerings to the temple granaries, and obedience to priestly injunctions, were viewed as the only ways to ward off divine wrath. The temples were usually the most prominent structures in Sumerian communities. Originally they were of modest proportions — one-room rectangular buildings made of the same mud brick the Sumerians used for their houses. But the temples were usually erected on platforms that raised them above their surroundings. Eventually, as communities prospered and grew, the temples also expanded, reaching skyward in stepped structures known as ziggurats.

Ziggurats originated in the process of temple rebuilding. Whenever the mud-brick walls of a temple collapsed from age or accident, the ruins served as the foundation for a new temple. As this renewal continued over the centuries, the sequence of one

building rising on the ruins of another came to resemble a series of giant steps. Sumerian architects eventually appropriated this stepped design, using it to build larger and grander temples that loomed above the Sumerian plain.

These towering ziggurats were no less magnificent inside. Sumerian artists portrayed their fellow citizens in painted frescoes and exquisite sculptures that adorned the walls of the temples' many rooms. Most of the men depicted in these scenes had long, curling beards and long hair parted in the middle; they frequently went bare chested and sported kiltlike garments that were drawn in severely at the waist. The women wore their hair in braids coiled around the head; they were dressed in form-fitting gowns that fastened at the shoulders and exposed only the right arm.

The Sumerian god of water, Enki (above, right), is portrayed in this seal impression with fish streaming about his shoulders. Because the Sumerians lived in fear of both prolonged droughts and severe floods, Enki was one of the most important of all deities, often glorified in sculpture and sacred verses. In one poem the god states: "When I draw near unto the yellowing fields, grain piles are heaped at my command." Also shown are winged Inanna, goddess of love and war, and the sun god, Utu, whose torso rises from behind a mountain range.

As the temples grew larger, their influence also burgeoned. Temples owned sizable tracts of land. Some of this acreage the priests farmed; some they gave to high government officials to curry political favor; and other tracts they rented out in return for a share of the crop. These harvests, together with crops contributed by farmers anxious to propitiate the gods who watched over their fields, gave the priesthood great economic leverage. The temple granary supported the priests themselves and any others who were deemed in special need — widows and orphaned children among them.

Feeding just those in the temple was no small task, for the ecclesiastical staffs continued to expand steadily over the centuries. The largest temples found it necessary to have both an administrator to keep the building and finances in good order and a spiritual leader — a high priest or priestess — to tend to less worldly matters. Next in rank came priests or priestesses whose duties included conducting the daily ceremonial offerings of food and drink to the temple's primary deity or praising that god with song and instrumental music.

But this was only the beginning. Increasingly, as the economy of Sumer grew, temples came to resemble miniature cities. In addition to the priests and other figures involved in religious rites, a temple housed corps of singers and musicians. There was a household staff that included cooks, maids, weavers, and courtyard sweepers. Small armies of field workers, many of whom were slaves, toiled in the temple's fields and granaries; secular officials administered the temple's various agricultural enterprises. Local artisans contracted with the temple to provide pottery, furniture, metal implements, and other goods. The bounty of the temple was enormous; for example, soon after 3000 BC, the temple in the city of Lagash was providing a daily bread and beer ration for no fewer than 1,200 people.

A goddess worshipped by the Mesopotamians wears a skirt decorated with fish swimming amid the undulating lines of a flowing river. Installed in the palace at Mari, a city-state on the upper Euphrates, this statuette was in fact a fountain: Water carried by pipe from a raised tank spouted from the vessel held in the goddess's hands.

Hardly less important than the priesthood in Sumerian society were traveling merchants — yet another sort of specialist produced by agricultural surpluses. Traders bartered Sumer's excess grain and wool for the raw materials that this land of plenty lacked completely.

Trading expeditions used all manner of conveyances. To bring lumber and stone downriver from the north, traders lashed the timbers together to make rafts, increased the flotation with inflated animal skins, and then loaded on the heavy cargo. Other merchants led donkey caravans through Syria to the Mediterranean coast and eastward through the passes of the Zagros Mountains into the lands of the Elamite tribes. They navigated the Persian Gulf in sailboats — probably another Sumerian invention — making their way into the Arabian Sea as far south as Oman. Eventually, some traders traveled as far east as the valley of the Indus River.

These intrepid merchants brought back not only such raw materials as ores, stone, and timber but also exotic items — ivory combs from the Indus Valley and carnelian beads from Elam — that added variety and excitement to Sumerian bazaars. In addition, the traders dealt in a less tangible but no less significant commodity — ideas. They expanded the intellectual horizons of the Sumerians by bringing home tales of foreign peoples who spoke strange languages and practiced unusual customs. In the same way, they opened minds in those other lands, leaving behind the stamp of the Sumerian way of doing things.

From the needs of religion, commerce, and government arose Sumer's most extraordinary achievement: the invention of writing. The priests found that they required a method of record keeping — a way to keep track of which farmers had made their annual contributions of barley to the temple granaries. Traders had to list what foodstuffs had been sent off to a foreign land for barter. Administrators wanted records of land surveys and civic activities. To preserve this information, scribes used sharpened reeds to etch marks in small tablets made of Sumer's most abundant raw material, clay. They worked on the clay when it was damp and soft; when it dried, the marks were ineradicable. What the early scribes etched on the tablets were pictographs — deftly rendered sketches of familiar everyday objects and creatures, such as sheaves of barley and oxen. They also drew people. The messages conveyed by these picture-words were for the most part simple and straightforward, dealing with such mundane matters as how much grain was involved in a transaction.

The Sumerian pictographs probably evolved from an even more primitive system of representation. As early as 8000 BC, small clay tokens of various distinctive shapes evidently were being used by Middle Eastern farmers to keep inventory of their commodities. A cone-shaped token, for example, might have indicated that a farmer had a certain amount of barley in his granary. Much later, merchants adopted the system of using tokens to serve as a kind of bill of lading to accompany goods being bought and sold. The tokens were placed in hollow clay balls known as *bullae,* and the balls were sealed. The merchant then scratched a numerical sign on the bulla to indicate how many tokens it contained.

The Sumerians found clay tablets to be far superior to the elaborate ball-and-token system. On the tablet, a merchant etched a numerical sign to indicate the amount of goods bought or sold; beside it, to specify the kind of commodity, he simply drew a picture of the token. The pictographs that emerged from this process underwent an immensely important evolution as time went on. From a concrete representation of

Seated in a courtyard below the ziggurat of Ur, a scribe records the donation of a sack of grain to the temple of the moon god Nanna, chief deity of the ziggurat complex. Such offerings — required of those who worked the land owned by the temple — went to support a host of its functionaries including weavers, metalworkers, potters, and carpenters. With a bureaucratic thoroughness characteristic of the Sumerians, each offering to the temple was acknowledged twice on clay tablets: One tablet went to the donor as a receipt, and the other was deposited in the sacred archives.

familiar objects, the writing system moved toward increasing abstraction. Combinations of pictographic symbols came to stand for certain ideas. For example, a picture of a mouth next to the wavy-line symbol for water meant "to drink." Then Sumerian scribes began to experiment with phonetic symbols, using a form of punning. The written symbol for one word came to represent another that sounded the same but had a different meaning.

Eventually, the picture-signs stood for sounds and ideas rather than for concrete objects. This system was so versatile that with a written vocabulary of about 600 characters — less than one-third that of the earlier pictographic language — Sumerian scribes could express in writing virtually anything that could be described in their spoken language.

The sculpted figure at left, dressed in the tufted wool skirt characteristic of Mesopotamia, is Ebih-il, steward of the Temple of Ishtar at Mari around the year 2400 BC. Such statues of devout men and women were housed in a sanctuary *(above)* — their hands folded in supplication to the god or goddess represented at the altar. Some shrines also held exquisite terra-cotta models of two-story dwellings, which probably served as offering tables.

As the content of Sumerian writing evolved, so did format and style. In the first pictographic tablets, the images were etched in vertical columns beginning in the top right corner. This proved awkward, however, because the scribe's hand often smudged previously incised signs. Scribes eventually found it more convenient to follow the method that later became standard in Western languages: writing in horizontal rows from left to right.

The scribes also grew dissatisfied with their writing tool. As the pointed stylus was drawn across the soft surface of the clay, it raised unsightly bumps and ridges. By 2500 BC, the reed point had taken on a triangular shape that could handily be pushed into the clay, leaving a neat, wedge-shaped impression. Clusters of these impressions made up the written symbols, which became increasingly stylized and abstract and less and less like the old pictographs that had directly shown the object being named. Much later, the configuration of the marks also gave to the Sumerian system of writing a name — cuneiform, from the Latin for "wedge-shaped."

Confined at first to the temple or the palace, writing spread rapidly through all areas of Sumerian society and then to other lands. Cuneiform script proved to be adaptable to many languages. As late as the century after the birth of Christ, a version of it was still being used by the Akkadian-speaking successors to the Sumerians in Mesopotamia.

In Sumer, cuneiform tablets were used to record codes of law promulgated by rulers; military commanders seized upon this new means of communication to pass orders on the battlefield. Poets began to inscribe in clay the old myths and stories that had previously been transmitted only by recitation or chant to the accompaniment of harp or lyre.

Supreme among the works of Sumerian literature were collections of these myths and tales that were rewritten into epics. None gained wider readership than the *Epic of Gilgamesh,* a 3,500-line poem that had its beginnings in fact; King Gilgamesh was a real ruler of the city of Uruk. *Gilgamesh* and other Sumerian tales foreshadowed themes found later in the Bible and in the literature of classical Greece. Gilgamesh himself, like Homer's Odysseus, wanders the earth — the first of world literature's great seekers. Another Sumerian myth presents a character who, like the biblical Noah, survived a great flood.

Other writing anticipated a more prosaic form of literature, the manual of practical advice. A dozen clay tablets and fragments discovered close to the city of Nippur constitute, for example, what could be called the world's first farmer's almanac. "In days of yore," it begins, "a farmer gave instructions to his son." There follow more than 100 lines devoted to providing advice on how to succeed in agriculture. Among the various precautions set out for the neophyte farmer is an admonishment for him to protect young seedlings from harm by saying a prayer to Ninkilim, the goddess of field mice and vermin. He is urged not to delay at harvest time until the barley bends under its own weight but to cut it at that mystical right moment — "in the day of its strength."

The author of this useful tract was almost certainly not a farmer. Most farmers, like other Sumerians, were illiterate. Learning to read and write cuneiform script required many years of rigorous training in the Sumerian school, or *edubba* — the world's first center of formal education.

The edubba (tablet house) was established as an annex to the temple or the royal palace for the purpose of training scribes. Tuition paid by the students maintained the headmaster, the *ummia* (expert or professor), and the teachers, who were known as "big brothers."

The students tended to come from high-ranking and wealthy families and, from all available evidences, were male. They attended the edubba from early youth to early manhood. Their very first lessons involved copying signs and committing to memory extended lists of related words and phrases. One list consisted of the names of animals, another of the parts of the body, and yet another of objects made of wood. When students mastered these primers sufficiently to reproduce hundreds of proper signs by heart, they advanced to a study of grammar and eventually to writing sentences, stories, and finally contracts and other practical documents.

The work was monotonous and the discipline harsh. One edubba student wrote of being beaten with a rod at least four times in a single day. His transgressions included loitering in the street, talking without permission, and failing to press cuneiform signs into the soft clay with sufficient skill to satisfy his "big brother."

If teachers were loath to spare the rod, they nonetheless seem to have been susceptible to flattery and outright bribery. A story written by an anonymous schoolteacher about 2000 BC tells an age-old tale of human frailty: A student, tired of being caned for various infractions at the edubba, urges his father to invite the teacher home. "To that which the schoolboy said, his father gave heed. The teacher was brought from school, and after entering the house he was seated in the place of honor. The schoolboy attended and served him, and whatever he had learned of the art of tablet writing he unfolded to his father."

Then the father takes over. Dressing the teacher "in a new garment," he presents a gift to him and puts a ring on his hand. The teacher is so overcome by this generosity that he forgets the boy's misbehavior and all those beatings. "You have carried out well the school's activities," he tells the lad. "You have become a man of learning." The story proved so popular that no fewer than twenty-one copies have been found.

In addition to perfecting their cuneiform script by copying such stories and various sorts of documents, aspiring scribes received a healthy dose of mathematics. The Sumerian system of calculation was based on the number sixty, a method that made practical sense because sixty can be divided by twelve numbers. It was therefore adapted for determining how food was to be allocated and for subdividing land; and Sumerian students honed their sexagesimal skills by solving practical problems such as the calculation of wages.

The Sumerian system may have been the forerunner of today's Arabic decimal system. In any event, traces of it survive in such familiar manifestations as the sixty-minute hour and the 360-degree circle.

Perseverance through the rigors of the edubba brought a handsome reward. Graduation assured the student employment and a place among the privileged. He might work in a temple or for the government as an accountant, a secretary, or an archivist, or he might gain a place in foreign trade.

The newly trained scribe could even set himself up in private practice, charging fees to write letters and legal agreements for illiterate clients. Such documents were made legal when clients signed the clay with their own unique seals. Such seals were minuscule works of art — small, cylindrical pieces of hard stone engraved all around with pictographs identifying the owner. When rolled in soft clay — a tablet or the clay used to seal a jar — the seal produced a frieze of repeated impressions that constituted the owner's legal signature. Every Sumerian adult, even if illiterate, therefore had the ability to write his or her name with exquisite style.

During the thrust toward civilization, Sumerian communities underwent profound physical changes. The dozen or so cities each contained several thousand inhabitants around 3000 BC. Five centuries later, the population of all Sumer exceeded 500,000, and an estimated four-fifths of the people lived in cities, where they congregated to seek the opportunities and amenities of the new urban way of life as well as protection from foreign marauders and invaders.

The cities evolved into even larger governmental jurisdictions — city-states — that grew to embrace the agricultural villages lying at their periphery. The first of these city-states, Uruk, became the prototype for others in the ancient world. In 2700 BC, Uruk included seventy-six outlying villages; the city itself sprawled over more than 1,000 acres and housed nearly 50,000 people. As protection against enemies, Uruk was surrounded by a wall six miles long and made of burnt brick that, according to the *Epic of Gilgamesh,* glistened in the harsh Sumerian sun "with the brilliance of copper."

That wall was a sign of the times, for warfare had become chronic in Sumer. Part of the reason was geography. Mesopotamia presented no natural barriers to invasion by the barbarous peoples who flanked it to the east and west. But an even more fruitful source of conflict lay in the disputes that flared between the Sumerian cities themselves. As the cities expanded, the citizens quarreled about their common boundaries and, with increasing frequency, about diversion of water from the rivers for irrigation. Every new canal dug upstream lessened the amount of water available to the cities downriver. Given the importance of irrigation, a dispute about water was often quite literally a matter of life and death.

The perennial hostilities wrought changes in the way Sumerians governed themselves. Until about 2800 BC, councils composed of aristocratic elders had made the important decisions in the cities. In times of crisis such as war, the council appointed a single leader, a *lugal,* which literally meant "big man." He led the community for the duration of the emergency, then returned as an honored hero to his former occupation. As the intervals of peace grew shorter, the lugal tended to stay in power for longer periods of time. Inevitably, he extended his authority as military commander to govern all phases of community life, superseding the council of elders that had originally appointed him. The word *lugal* came to mean "king." In time, one lugal after another took it upon himself to appoint his successor. Thus were born the various dynasties that thereafter ruled the Sumerian city-states.

The power of the kings grew to rival that of the temples, but the city-state sovereigns were careful to maintain cordial relations with the priests. Even when a monarchy was solidly entrenched, the king sought the approval and support of the priests — and in

A CITY FOR THE MOON GOD

Seen here in the light of a new day, the Sumerian city of Ur was one of the great metropolises of the third millennium BC. Near its center was a sprawling temple complex, where a mud-brick ziggurat, dedicated to the moon god Nanna and his wife Ningal, rose some eighty feet in three stepped terraces. Surrounding the holy precinct was the city, a warren of houses, shops, and bazaars — home to more than 30,000 people.

Two broad canals circumscribed Ur, connecting it with the nearby Euphrates and thence to the Persian Gulf. A third waterway cut through the heart of the city. Among the vessels moored in the city's two placid harbors were foreign ships, come to trade with Ur's artisans and farmers. Beyond the city's thick walls lay the plain of the Euphrates, a patchwork of cultivated fields laced together by irrigation canals and ditches. Those who worked these plots saw the city as a sanctuary. Its ramparts frustrated invaders, and its elevation above the swampy plain — produced by years of building on the ruins of abandoned structures — provided security from the constant threat of floods. The city's towering ziggurat was a beacon: From as far as twenty miles away, a peasant could look up from his hoe, see the so-called heavenly mountain, and be assured of Nanna's protection.

return was considered to be the deity's earthly representative, a ruler by divine right. The semidivine status of the king of Ur was sanctified by a number of rituals, the most important occurring on New Year's Day. On that occasion, the king ascended in solemn procession to the top of the city's principal ziggurat, where a symbolic marriage was performed, uniting him, as a substitute for one of the gods, to a priestess who represented Inanna, the goddess of fertility.

The kings greatly expanded the activities of the city-state governments, which undertook massive public-works programs such as digging new canals, enlarging the temples, and constructing roads. Some cities even possessed rudimentary postal services. Inevitably, bureaucracies came into being to handle the increased amount of civic activities. There were soon overseers, inspectors, tax collectors, and scribes to put everything in writing.

Chief among the king's myriad responsibilities was the promulgation and the administration of laws. Even before kingship became the accepted form of government, individuals had been drawing up legal agreements, a process that began at least as early as 2700 BC and, like cuneiform writing itself, was rooted in the needs of commerce. Tablets surviving from that time bear witness to transactions involving the sale of land, houses, and slaves.

As Sumerian society became more complex, the demand arose for uniform laws to govern not only commercial transactions but also civil and criminal conduct. The kings answered this need, issuing collections of laws. The earliest collection unearthed so far dates from the reign of Ur-Nammu, king of the city of Ur early in the twenty-first century. It was probably devised by Ur-Nammu's son, Shulgi. Written royal decrees must certainly have been handed down several centuries before that; even so, Ur-Nammu's set of laws precedes that far better known written guide to conduct, the biblical Ten Commandments, by about 1,000 years.

Only five of Ur-Nammu's laws can be read, because the sole surviving copy — a four-by-eight-inch clay tablet inscribed on both sides — is badly damaged. Three of those five rules are of special interest, however, because they seem to reflect a remarkably enlightened judicial philosophy. In an age when the ancient rule of "an eye for an eye" prevailed, Ur-Nammu's laws prescribed fines instead of corporal punishment or mutilation as the penalty for physical injury inflicted upon another person. One edict reads: "If a man has severed with a weapon the bones of another man, he shall pay one mina of silver." Sumer had exhibited typical originality, it appears, not only in codifying written laws, but also in making the laws humane.

The operation of the judicial system also seems to have been enlightened. There were no juries, but defendants were tried before a panel of several judges — usually elders selected from the community — and testimony was taken from witnesses under oath. Verdicts could be appealed to the king himself. Written laws and contracts played an important part not only in criminal justice and commerce but also in marriage. In the wedding ceremony, a scribe engraved a tablet with the agreed-upon marriage contract, and the bride and groom then signed it with their cylinder seals. The contract specified, among other provisions, the duties of each spouse and the penalties the husband would pay should he decide upon a divorce.

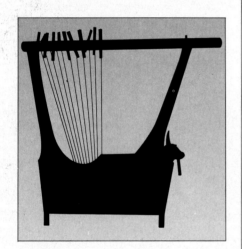

Affixed to a superbly crafted Sumerian lyre *(left)*, the golden bull's head detailed at right indicates the ritual function of the instrument, which was found in the royal cemetery at Ur. Bulls were symbols of strength and fertility, and the plaited beard on this creature — fashioned of lapis lazuli — may have been intended to be interpreted as a sign of divinity. Before plucking the strings of the lyre, musicians would wash their fingers to purify them, and many of the verses they sang were hymns to the gods. "They play the stringed instrument that brings joy to all people," wrote one Sumerian poet. "They play songs for Inanna to rejoice the heart."

Marriage was arranged by the parents, and the betrothal was legally recognized when the groom presented a gift of money to the bride's father — a vestige of an earlier custom in which the groom simply purchased the bride. The gift had the effect of making the betrothal more binding. If the young man broke the engagement, he forfeited the money. On the other hand, if the bride changed her mind, the disappointed groom could recover twice the amount.

Married or single, women had a number of important rights under Sumerian law. They could own property, engage in business, and qualify as witnesses in court. In other ways, however, they were second-class citizens. For example, the family was patrilineal: Property was handed down from father to son. And the rules of marriage seem to have been one-sided. By law and custom, the husband could take one or more concubines, divorce his wife if she proved barren, and even sell her into slavery for as long as three years to obtain money to pay off his debts.

Perhaps the most remarkable of all the surviving Sumerian documents relating to law is a tablet that preceded Ur-Nammu's collection of laws by about 200 years. This tablet tells a story that illuminates the notion of justice, describing reforms undertaken in the city-state of Lagash around the year 2350 BC by King Urukagina.

The document begins by recounting the worst abuses of the previous regime. High taxes and oppressive laws, originally put into effect because the city-state was engaged in war, had been carried over into peacetime. Tax collectors and other corrupt royal officials were everywhere, taking donkeys and sheep from farmers and even showing up at cemeteries to seize a portion of the bread and barley that families carried to furnish the graves of their recently deceased relatives.

According to the tablet, King Urukagina changed all this. He fired the dishonest tax collectors and other tainted officials, gave amnesty to citizens unjustly imprisoned, and most important, decreed ordinances protecting common citizens from exploitation by the government. In the unknown author's account of all this, there appears for the first time in recorded history the word *freedom*.

The entrenchment of the monarchy and the consequent expansion of government served to etch even deeper the lines that existed between the social classes. During the third millennium, three distinct classes emerged in Sumerian cities. At one extreme was the aristocracy: the king and his government officials, the most prominent priests, and the wealthiest merchants and landowners. At the other extreme were the slaves, forced to remain in bondage because of political or economic circumstances. In the middle was the great majority of the Sumerian populace — ordinary free citizens such as farmers, fishermen, artisans, and scribes.

The people at the top lived best, of course. The biggest landowners sometimes had estates covering hundreds of acres. Like the temples, many of these royal and provincial estates resembled small towns in their complexity: Workshops on the grounds turned out household goods; there were usually dormitories for artisans and slaves. The houses of the Sumerian well-to-do, whether on estates or in the cities, were usually comfortable structures that often contained a dozen or more rooms; in most homes, all the rooms opened through high arched doorways onto an interior courtyard. The inside brick walls usually were plastered with mud and whitewashed; reed matting or woven wool carpets covered the brick floors. Some houses had private rooms for worship, with brick altars. Recesses in the walls held clay statuettes of the households' special deities, who served as go-betweens to gods of loftier station.

No residence of the aristocracy could compare with that of the king. The palaces of rulers became increasingly lavish, rivaling even the towering ziggurats in size and elegance. The palace at Mari was spread out over more than eight acres and contained almost 300 rooms. In the midst of such splendor, the lugal conducted governmental affairs from his throne on a raised platform, received emissaries from other city-states, and enjoyed the music of harp and lyre, as well as specially composed hymns or poems that sang his praises.

The slaves labored in the palaces and temples and on the great estates. Some slaves were ordinary citizens who were being punished for a crime. Others were prisoners of war; in fact, the Sumerian word for *slave* derived from the term for *foreigner*. Because much of the warfare involved battles between the city-states, however, most of the prisoner-slaves were Sumerian.

Many slaves entered bondage voluntarily. Landless peasants, for example, sometimes sold themselves as slaves simply for meals and a place to sleep. Parents could legally sell their children into slavery. A man in desperate financial straits might turn over his entire family — himself included — to a creditor for an agreed-upon time in satisfaction of his debts.

Though slaves were legally the property of the master and could be branded, flogged, or otherwise severely punished for transgressions such as attempted escape, they too possessed certain rights. They could engage in business and borrow money. If a slave was married to a free spouse, any of their children were free from birth. Slaves could even buy their own freedom.

The way of life of those who made up the broad middle class varied enormously. The artisans who practiced their craft in the palaces or on the landed estates were dependent on those institutions for their food and clothing. Others rendered their services or exchanged their wares for money, usually a standard weight of silver — or for some other commodity — and maintained modest one-story houses on the narrow, winding city streets. Many other citizens, besides farmers, evidently possessed their own property, even if it was only a small plot for a garden.

For rich and poor, free citizen and slave alike, the staple of the diet was grain — sometimes wheat, but usually barley, which grew better in the alkaline and saline soils of Sumer. Kernels of barley were either beaten into coarse particles and cooked as a kind of porridge or ground into flour and baked into the unleavened bread that is still eaten throughout the Middle East.

Barley also was the principal ingredient for the most popular beverage, beer — or rather ale, since the preservative herbs such as hops that are used to make true beer would not be introduced for another 4,000 years. This ale was usually brewed by women in their homes and sold from there. A special goddess was believed to preside over the ale's preparation — Ninkasi, whose name literally means ''the lady who fills the mouth.''

The name was appropriate. About 40 percent of Sumerian grain production went into brewers' vats. The ordinary temple worker received a ration of two pints a day, and senior dignitaries qualified for five times that amount. The citizenry was so addicted to ale that the Greeks later insisted that even their own fun-loving god Dionysus had fled the land of Sumer in disgust.

For variety in the Sumerian diet, plenty of vegetables were available — chickpeas, lentils and beans, onions, and fresh green lettuce. And fish were available in profusion. Tablets list no fewer than fifty varieties of fish that were taken from the Tigris and the

Sumerian game board with pieces

As people of the pioneering civilizations acquired wealth and leisure, their games grew more elegant and complex. The Sumerian game board at top was fit for a king. Designed by a royal artisan at Ur, it was formed of squares of shell inlaid with lapis lazuli and red limestone; its pieces were kept in a drawer within the board. Players cast dice or threw sticks before moving their tokens; although the rules of the match have not survived, bringing one's men through the narrow pass must have been of strategic importance.

In time, offshoots of this game — with variously shaped boards of twenty squares — spread westward. The version shown at far right was introduced to Egypt from the Near East by the Hyksos, who overran the Nile Delta around 1650 BC. The Egyptians also came up with games of their own, including a contest in which vying teams of ivory hounds and jackals raced about a palm tree, their movements based on the roll of dice.

ANCIENT PASTIMES

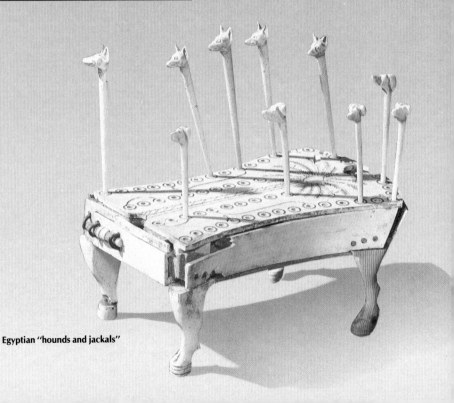

Egyptian "hounds and jackals"

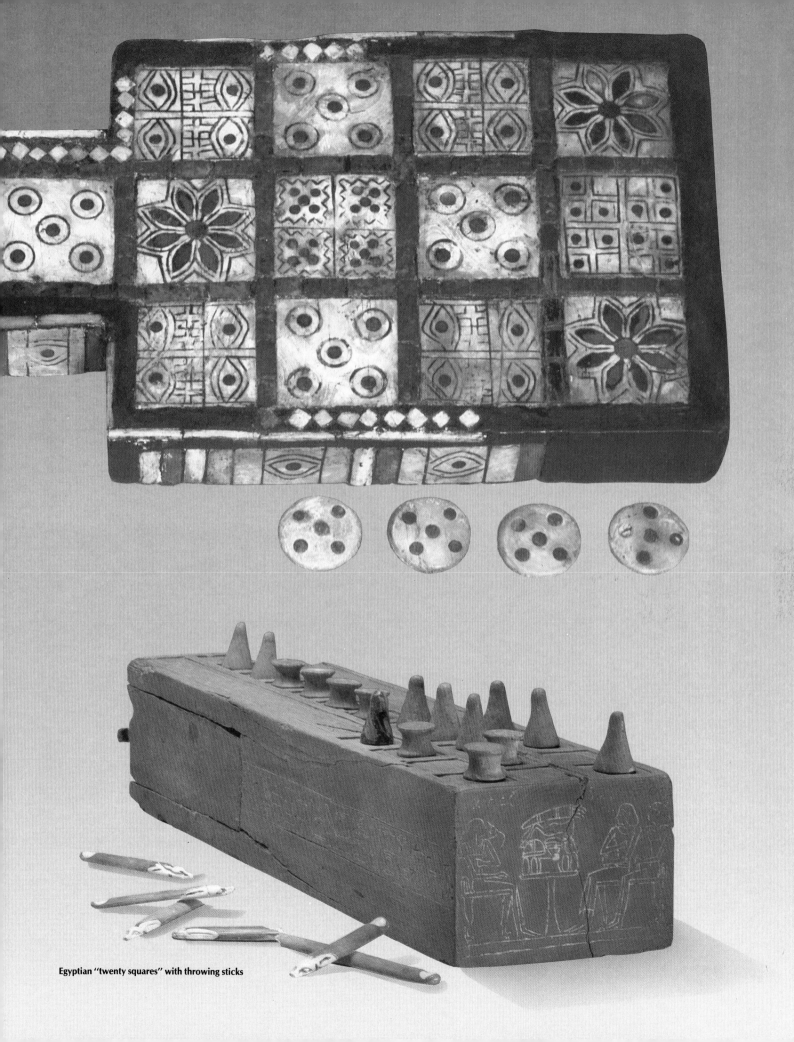

Egyptian "twenty squares" with throwing sticks

Euphrates rivers. In the streets of cities such as Ur, fish vendors were everywhere, some selling their stock fresh, others frying it for immediate consumption. Herds of cattle and goats were kept primarily for the milk they could provide, which was also made into cheese, butter, and yogurt. In all probability, only the wealthy ate meat with any regularity, and much of that was likely to have been mutton. The Sumerians may have descended from nomadic shepherds, for their language had more than 200 words describing the different kinds of sheep.

One of the most prolific providers of nourishment was the date palm. Clinging to the banks of the rivers and irrigation canals, growing both naturally and under cultivation, date palms yielded about 100 pounds of fruit per tree every year. Dates could be eaten fresh, dried for later use, or pressed into a thick syrup and used as an alternative to honey for sweetening. (Sugar was not yet known in the Middle East.) Even the stones of the fruit were put to use: They could be crushed to provide fodder for cattle or burned to make charcoal.

In matters of physical health, the Sumerians at first relied on spiritual remedies. Those who became ill usually turned to exorcists, who specialized in expunging the demons that were thought to be responsible for disease. But as early as 2500 BC, alternative treatment was available. By then, trained physicians had appeared, and they were able to prescribe a variety of nostrums.

Fifteen of the remedies employed by Sumerian physicians were recorded on a clay tablet. The prescriptions call for compounds of natural ingredients — plants, and minerals such as salt and saltpeter. Ale appears in many of the prescriptions, either as an active ingredient or as a palliative to make the medicine go down easier. One remedy, freely translated, advises the doctor: ''Pour strong ale over some resin; heat over a fire. Combine this liquid with river bitumen oil and let the sick man drink it.'' Unfortunately, the medical tablet fails to specify which ailments this and the other prescriptions

This military standard, a mosaic made for display in royal processions, details a successful campaign by troops of the powerful city-state of Ur around 2500 BC. At bottom, two-man chariots drawn by asses surge forward over the bodies of the enemy. One charioteer drives the team while the other hurls the spears carried in a rack at the front of the chariot. In the middle panel, prisoners are being pushed along by a phalanx of helmeted infantry troops. At top, the king stands in the center — flanked by his retinue, including a dwarflike groom — as enemy captives are brought before him to meet their fate. Masses of Sumerian prisoners of war were executed on the spot: Those spared were kept as slaves.

were intended to cure or alleviate. But several of the listed ingredients suggest that practical experience rather than mere superstition lay behind the remedies. Salt, for example, is an effective antiseptic, and saltpeter a good astringent. Two of the salves recorded on the tablet call for an alkali — probably soda ash — plus ingredients high in natural fat. Such a combination would produce soaplike substances that might have helped prevent infections.

Despite all the remedies and the best efforts of the exorcists, Sumerians went to an early grave. The average lifespan probably did not exceed forty years of age. For some people, the place of burial was close at hand. In many houses, a small brick vault was built beneath the ground floor, and it was used to inter members of the family when their time came. It was not uncommon for ten or more persons to be buried in these small mausoleums.

Other Sumerians were buried in graves in cemeteries outside the cities. No matter where the body was laid to rest, the ritual followed a pattern. The deceased was wrapped in reed matting or, much more rarely, placed in a coffin fashioned of wood or clay. The corpse was stretched out on its side, with a bowl of water between the hands and near the lips. A few treasured personal belongings — his weapons or tools, her jewelry — might go into the grave as well. And almost always, the family included several additional vessels full of food and drink to sustain the departed during the stay in another world — and to make sure that a hungry or thirsty spirit did not return to haunt the local streets and byways.

The quantity and quality of grave furnishings depended on a person's wealth and station. In death as in life, the most lavish trappings attended royalty. The royal tombs of Ur were vast pits containing burial chambers constructed of brick and stone and designed, perhaps for the first time in the history of building, with such sophisticated architectural forms as the arch, vault, and dome. The chamber held the body of the king and such personal effects as ceramic jewelry, figurines of lapis lazuli, bowls of gold and silver, and other consummate Sumerian accomplishments in metallurgy such as superbly gilded daggers.

Royal tombs were furnished not only with exquisite works of art but also in some instances with people. For a brief period in Sumerian history, it became the custom of members of a king's household — soldiers, musicians, ladies-in-waiting, grooms, and others — to be conducted with great ceremony into the burial pit and ritually sacrificed beside the vault of their deceased monarch. One excavated tomb contained no fewer than seventy-four people who had probably been poisoned or drugged to near-insensibility and had then been covered over where they fell. Perhaps they were supposed to attend the deceased in the afterlife as they had served him while he was alive.

Finally Sumer itself expired. Even as the people of the valley developed the traits and institutions that would constitute their great gift to humanity, they were nurturing the seeds of their own destruction. The tragic defect in the development of Sumerian civilization was the failure to live in peace — to resolve the bitter disputes between the city-states. For much of the third millennium, the plain between the rivers was ravaged by warfare. People who ought to have been united by a common language and culture instead hacked at one another with axes and maces, ran one another through with lances, pierced one another with daggers and arrows.

Most of the soldiers fighting for the various city-states appear to have been conscripts called up for the duration of the conflict. In such cases, those skilled in particular crafts such as carpentry or silversmithing often formed their own platoons under the command of their supervisor from civilian life. But some of the troops were professional soldiers. According to a clay tablet, one of the most powerful Sumerian kings, Sargon, had a household numbering 5,400 men — most of them presumably professional warriors — who "ate with him daily."

As the war-torn third millennium wore on, one city would win ascendancy in Sumer only to have it wrested away. During the early centuries of that millennium, supreme power seems to have shifted successively southward, from the city of Kish to Uruk and then to Ur. After about 2500 BC, the two main antagonists appear to have been Lagash, about thirty-five miles northeast of Uruk, and Umma, just a little farther north. The neighbors repeatedly fought over irrigation rights to the waters of the Tigris. Other city-states aligned themselves either with Lagash or Umma and formed rival alliances, thus expanding quarrels that once had been local in nature.

Something of the ruthlessness of Sumerian warfare during this period is conveyed by surviving fragments of what came to be known as the Stela of the Vultures, a stone monument erected about 2450 BC in Lagash by King Eannatum to commemorate a victory over Umma. One scene on the monument shows the king, clad in a kilt and a loose-fitting upper garment, leading his troops into battle. His soldiers, wearing copper helmets and armed with pikes and axes, form a phalanx of six close ranks protected by a front rank of men carrying large rectangular shields.

Other scenes on the monument depict the brutal aftermath of the battle, the soldiers of Lagash slaughtering the enemy prisoners while vultures fly away from the field carrying in their beaks the severed heads of the vanquished. In this fight, the victor Eannatum claimed to have killed 3,600 of the enemy while burying "twenty heaps" of his own dead.

But Eannatum, who briefly grasped dominion over the whole of Sumer, soon went down in battle; a few generations later, about 2375 BC, the neighboring city he had humiliated got its revenge. Umma's new ruler, Lugalzaggesi, invaded Lagash, slaughtering its citizens and burning its temples. Lugalzaggesi then overran several other important cities, including Sumer's chief religious center, Nippur, before suffering a crushing defeat. He ended his days locked in a pillory at the gate of Nippur where those he had once ruled could walk by and revile him.

The conqueror of Lugalzaggesi — indeed of all Sumer — was Sargon the Great, one of the most extraordinary figures of his time. Born about 2335 BC, Sargon was not of Sumerian ancestry, but the son of Semites — a people who had long been drifting eastward into the region between the Tigris and the Euphrates from the deserts of the Arabian Peninsula. The Semites settled in Sumer and in the land just north of it, which came to be called Akkad — and they, Akkadians.

The precise location and circumstances of Sargon's birth are unknown, although numerous legends have sought to illuminate his childhood. According to one Moses-like story, his mother put the baby, who was illegitimate, in a pitch-covered basket and entrusted him to fate by launching the frail craft down the Euphrates. A Sumerian farmer drawing water to irrigate his field found the basket and reared the child as his own. From these humble circumstances, it was said, Sargon somehow rose to become a high official — cupbearer to the king of Kish, Sumer's northernmost city.

Whatever the truth of these traditions, Sargon embarked on a remarkable series of military campaigns. After putting Lugalzaggesi in the pillory, he marched his pha-

Battle scenes carved on a pair of stones demonstrate that the Sumerians were fierce warriors with little appetite for compromise or clemency. Above, the bearded god Ningirsu, patron of the city-state of Lagash, brings his mace down on the skull of a prisoner held in a net with other captives; the tableau commemorates the victory of Lagash over its bitter rival, Umma. At right, with bow in hand, King Naram-Sin, grandson of the great warrior-king Sargon, looms over his abject opponents — tribesmen known as the Lullubi, who met defeat in the Zagros Mountains, east of the Tigris.

33

lanxes of lancers and archers and his donkey-drawn war chariots against the other major cities of Sumer. Then he pivoted in a mighty counterclockwise sweep: east to conquer the troublesome Elamites, north to gain control of Akkad and the rest of upper Mesopotamia, and then west across the desert to extend the range of his conquests to the Mediterranean.

For the first time, all of Mesopotamia was united as a single nation under one ruler. Somewhere along the Euphrates River in Akkad — its site remains unknown — Sargon established a new capital called Agade, which numerous tablets describe as being one of the most magnificent cities ever built in the ancient world. From Agade, Sargon governed his newly won empire with singular verve and imagination for more than fifty years, deploying his troops to strategic outposts and appointing his fellow Akkadians to important administrative positions in the city-states.

Sumer, although politically in the grip of Akkad, imposed its cultural will on the Semitic conquerors. The Akkadians borrowed from the Sumerians not only their irrigation techniques but also their cuneiform writing and their entire pantheon of gods. And everywhere that Sargon went with his army, he transplanted the seeds of Sumerian civilization.

The dynasty that had been founded by Sargon lasted less than a century before breaking up under the impact of internal conflict and invasion by another group of aggressive foreigners. From the Zagros Mountains to the northeast came the Gutians — "a people which brooks no controls," as they were described on a Sumerian tablet. These invaders sacked Sargon's capital city of Agade, set up a loosely organized rule over the northern plains around Umma, and began assimilating Sumerian culture. The Sumerians put up with these bumptious outsiders for less than half a century before initiating a series of uprisings that drove the Gutians from their land.

The stage was now set in the cities of the plain for one last gasp of Sumerian political autonomy. Around 2100 BC, the enlightened Ur-Nammu founded the final dynasty of Sumerian kings. That dynasty's birth was not auspicious, however. Ur-Nammu had ascended the throne through treachery, having deposed King Utuhegal, hero of the anti-Gutian rebellion, who had unwisely entrusted Ur-Nammu with the governorship of Ur.

Nevertheless, Ur-Nammu turned out to be a superb leader. Ruling from the city of Ur, which by then had a population of nearly 40,000, he reunited Sumer by dint of political guile and military muscle. In addition to promulgating his collection of laws, he presided over a renaissance in commerce, the arts, and architecture. He ordered the renovation of irrigation canals that had fallen into disrepair and built in Ur the biggest and most magnificent ziggurat in the land — a temple tower 200 feet wide at its base and soaring 70 feet above the plain. Ur-Nammu also made certain that posterity would know of his good works: Each brick in the ziggurat bore a stamp of his name.

But even then, when Sumer seemed at the pinnacle of its power, the foundations of its civilization were beginning to crumble. Its very underpinning, agriculture, was falling into decline because centuries of irrigation had finally diminished the fertility of the fields, leaving residues of salt as the water evaporated. Crop production dwindled, surplus food stocks were expended, and anxiety haunted Sumer. The city-states, their political strength already sapped by a millennium of squabbling and fighting, soon lapsed into the old pattern of warring among themselves.

Then came stepped-up pressure from the barbarian tribes that bordered Sumer.

King Sargon of Akkad, majestically portrayed here in a bronze sculpture from around 2300 BC, was a man of humble origins — the son of an unknown wanderer, some surmised. Yet he played his hand masterfully, placing all Mesopotamia under his rule. Once his forces had broken down the walls of Ur, he established his daughter there as high priestess. She later composed a tribute to the fierce goddess Ishtar that could have been addressed as well to her father: "At your roar you made the countries bow low."

About 1950 BC, those old enemies on the east, the Elamites, took advantage of Sumer's weakened state, invading and destroying the city of Ur. They carried its king off into captivity and toppled the dynasty founded by Ur-Nammu a century earlier. Next, from the deserts to the west, appeared a new enemy, the Amorites. Semitic nomads who raised cattle and herded sheep, the Amorites had been peacefully infiltrating Sumer for years, even serving as mercenaries in the armies of the various city-states. Now they entered Mesopotamia in even greater numbers, overrunning the cities and eventually establishing their capital in the north, at the hitherto unimportant town of Babylon. There, while the Sumerians were engaged in fighting each other farther south, the Amorites founded a dynasty of kings.

Babylon still had not accomplished much before the sixth in this line of kings, Hammurabi, took his place on the throne shortly after 1800 BC. At the time, his dominion extended no more than fifty miles from the city. But with cunning, courage, and inexhaustible energy, Hammurabi effected great changes during a remarkable reign of forty-two years.

Hammurabi's best-known legacy is his collection of laws. Preserved as engravings on a seven-foot-high monument of black diorite, the Code of Hammurabi lists close to 300 royal legal decisions. They relate to civil matters, such as workers' wages, and describe penalties for criminal offenses ranging from felling a neighbor's date palm without his consent to committing murder. Although evidently influenced by Sumerian law and custom, these penalties also reflect the much harsher Amorite tradition. Female adultery, for example, is dealt with summarily: "If the wife of a man has been caught while lying with another man, they shall be bound and cast into the water."

But Hammurabi's legal achievements paled by comparison with his political and military accomplishments. Making alliances and then breaking them when it suited him, molding his Amorites into a disciplined army, he took on the quarreling city-states of Sumer and conquered them one by one. In short order, he succeeded in welding Sumer and northern Mesopotamia into a single nation. His forging of the Babylonian empire marked the end of Sumer politically — but not culturally. Like Sargon and the Akkadians before them, Hammurabi and his Amorites simply swallowed Sumerian civilization whole. Borrowing virtually everything except the Sumerian language, they absorbed the writing, art, literature, educational system, and — with a change or two — even the religion of the vanquished.

Under Babylonian rule, the last of the Sumerian poets sorrowfully jabbed cuneiform sticks into soft clay, pouring out lamentations for the political demise of their land. Yet in the very act of writing, they were ensuring that the ideas and ideals of Sumer would not die but would leave their wedge-shaped marks on future civilizations, enriching many cultures through the centuries to come.

THE POWER OF THE WRITTEN WORD

The first revolution in human communication occurred when the Sumerians — and shortly thereafter the Egyptians — developed written languages. This step had stupendous impact. With writing, humans could record their deeds and transactions, give lasting form to their thoughts and visions, and preserve their laws and commandments. Writing proved a mighty goad to progress and vastly speeded the growth and spread of civilization.

The Sumerian system of writing went through several developmental stages, a number of them roughly paralleled by the Egyptian. The first stage in Sumerian writing was clearly pictorial, with picture-symbols standing for concrete objects and actions. A stylized drawing of a human head meant "head"; two wavy lines meant "water."

But quite soon this limited system was extended by making certain pictures stand for less easily communicated words. The Sumerian sign for "mouth" also came to mean "speak." In a short time, the system was expanded again by the combination of symbols: A literate Sumerian of about 2800 BC knew that the linked signs for "mouth" and "food" meant the verb "to eat."

The greatest change took place when the picture-symbols in large measure came to stand for sounds — generally the sounds that began the words the pictures had previously stood for. The transformation was far from complete; many Sumerian characters and Egyptian hieroglyphs retained their

A message signed "your loving wife who has had a child" appears on a bit of clay.

picture meanings. But by about 2400 BC, both writing systems represented most of the sounds of the spoken languages.

As the functions of many of the written symbols changed, so did their appearance. The formal Egyptian hieroglyphs, suitable for incision on stone monuments and temples, gave birth to a less pictorial script called hieratic, which was better suited to writing with ink on paperlike papyrus. The simple pictographs that early Sumerian scribes had scratched in their clay tablets became highly stylized characters.

In addition, the uses made of writing tended to change over the years. Most early Sumerian tablets record practical matters, such as lists of agricultural produce. In time, literate people would begin to communicate in more intimate ways, setting down tender domestic messages like the one above. Far weightier tasks occupied other scribes: royal decrees, law codes, works of literature. Even the most mundane of these applications, however, testifies to a huge imaginative leap: Humans had found a way to make permanent their perishable thoughts, to carry them across space to distant places and across time to all succeeding generations. Many cultures would evolve their own scripts in the centuries to come, but the next revolution in communications, the invention of printing, would not take place for almost 5,000 years.

An accounting of food-stuffs, written before 3000 BC, includes some of the picture-symbols in the chart at right, such as "to eat" *(lower left corner)*.

	3300 BC	2800 BC	2400 BC	1800 BC
HEAVEN				
EARTH				
MALE				
FEMALE				
MOUNTAIN				
MAN				
GREAT				
KING				
PLOW				
GRAIN				
SHEEP				
OX				
FISH				
BIRD				
HEAD				
MOUTH				
WATER				
TO DRINK				
FOOD				
TO EAT				
HAND				
FOOT				

The selection of Sumerian written characters included in the chart at right shows the gradual mutations that the script underwent during a period of 1,500 years, as early pictographs were transformed into a system of abstract symbols.

A number of the pictographs employed about 3300 BC *(column two)* can readily be understood. The rays of a star denoted heaven and, by extension, a deity. A bowl clearly meant "food." In some, the combined symbols are immediately intelligible: The pictographs for "great" and "man" logically added up to "king."

The first step toward abstraction came after 3000 BC, when the pictographs were turned on their side *(column three)*, a change that may have resulted when Sumerian scribes began to rotate their tablets and write from left to right, rather than from top to bottom. Whatever the reason for the shift, it meant that the symbols now bore less of a resemblance to the thing signified.

A more radical change occurred after scribes turned from drawing on the soft clay with a sharpened reed to the use of a stylus with a wedge-shaped point. Impressing the clay with a stylus yielded a unique script *(column four)*, later called cuneiform after the Latin *cuneus,* or "wedge." By 1800 BC, scribes had simplified many cuneiform characters to produce still more abstract symbols that only remotely resemble pictographs.

FROM PICTURE TO SYMBOL

The Sumerian tablet at right, dating from about 2350 BC, lists in columns the livestock and animal skins delivered to a temple in Lagash. Among the cuneiform signs are "sheep" and "male" in the top right segment.

A portable tablet lists the bread and other rations carried by Sumerian couriers about 2100 BC.

Inserted upside down, a tablet is shielded by a clay envelope that itself has been inscribed with cuneiform characters. Both the inner and outer texts concern a legal case, the division of property between a man named Abban and his sister Bittatti, that was heard before King Niqmepa during the eighteenth century BC. Although the symbols are derived from those used by the Sumerians, the language they express is old Akkadian, the tongue spoken by a people who ruled much of Mesopotamia after 2350 BC.

The shape of this model sheep's liver evidently revealed a dire omen. The sentence on the left side foretells the "destruction of small towns."

The Sumerians and later the Akkadian-speaking Babylonians and Assyrians put the cuneiform script to a remarkable variety of uses, from the exalted to the mundane. Royalty, the priesthood, merchants, and teachers all relied on writing, as illustrated by the various inscribed tablets and objects shown here and on the next four pages. At left is a clay model of a sheep's liver, which — in addition to the real organ — was employed to teach apprentice priests the art of divination. More practical for everyday use were the student's geometry textbook *(below)*; the measure of weight *(bottom right)*; and the medical tract *(far right)*, which offers remedies for a variety of ills.

A large fragment of a mathematics exercise tablet, dating from about 1700 BC, combines geometric shapes with questions written in Akkadian. The text in the lower right corner loosely translates as: "The side of the square equals one. I have drawn four triangles in it. What is the surface area?" How to solve such problems was taught in Sumerian and Babylonian schools to young scribes who would be required to draw up accurate deeds and calculate agricultural yields.

THE MULTIPURPOSE SCRIPT

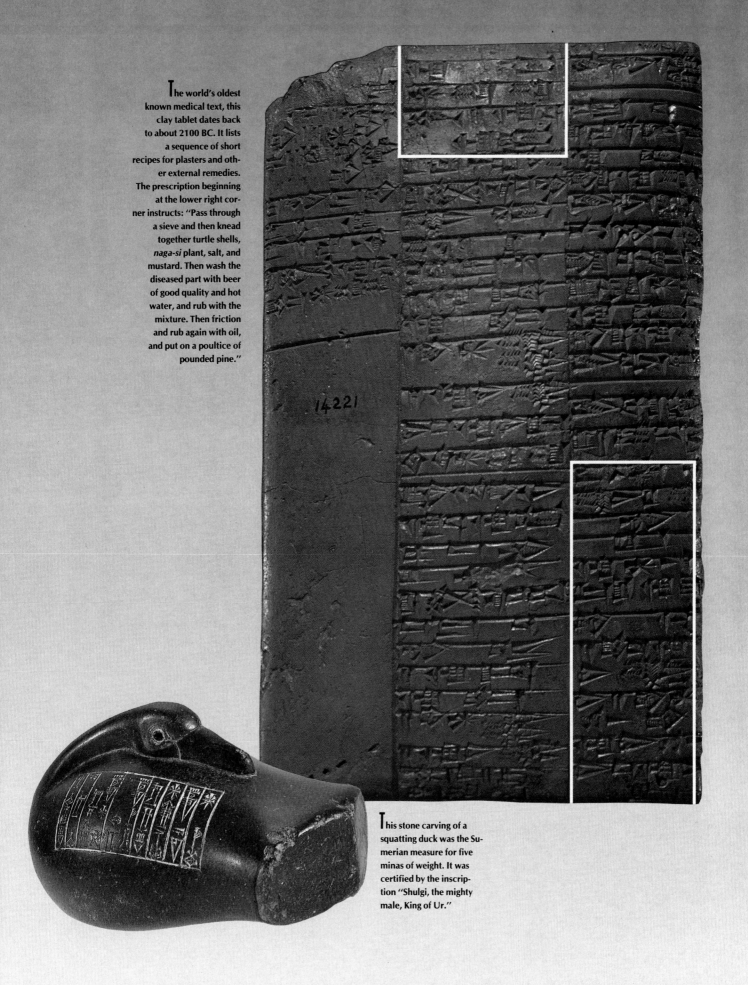

The world's oldest known medical text, this clay tablet dates back to about 2100 BC. It lists a sequence of short recipes for plasters and other external remedies. The prescription beginning at the lower right corner instructs: "Pass through a sieve and then knead together turtle shells, *naga-si* plant, salt, and mustard. Then wash the diseased part with beer of good quality and hot water, and rub with the mixture. Then friction and rub again with oil, and put on a poultice of pounded pine."

This stone carving of a squatting duck was the Sumerian measure for five minas of weight. It was certified by the inscription "Shulgi, the mighty male, King of Ur."

The Sumerians often used writing to make clear the significance of the statuettes they placed in temples as offerings to their deities. The cuneiform on the skirt of the figure at right indicates that he represents King Gudea, ruler of Lagash around 2150 BC, and that the potentate had dedicated not only this image, but also an entire temple, to the goddess Geshtin-anna.

The writing on this copper religious figurine — made about 2100 BC — records that the mighty King Ur-Nammu constructed a temple for the goddess Inanna "and restored it as it should be." Such small figures were frequently buried in the foundations of buildings as dedicatory offerings.

Among the world's earliest historical documents is this list of Sumerian kings, written about 1820 BC on a four-sided clay block. The highlighted section reads: "Uruk was smitten with weapons; its kingship was carried to Ur. In Ur, Ur-Nammu became king and reigned eighteen years. Shulgi, son of divine Ur-Nammu, reigned forty-eight years; divine Amar-Sin, son of divine Shulgi, reigned nine years; Shu-Sin, son of divine Amar-Sin, reigned nine years, and Ibbi-Sin, son of Shu-Sin, reigned twenty-four years."

The inscription on this clay cone from Lagash, once driven into a mud-brick wall as decoration, thanked the god Ningir-su, who was credited with settling a bitter border dispute with a nearby town.

1923.444

The story of Atra-hasis, hero of one of the world's first epics, is written in Akkadian cuneiform on the tablet below. A portion of the tale describes a great flood, comparable to the deluge in the Bible's Book of Genesis. Having been warned by a god that "it will rain down upon you a profusion of fishes," Atra-hasis built a strong ark amply caulked with pitch and rode out the catastrophe.

Sampled at right, the comprehensive set of laws promulgated by the Babylonian king Hammurabi is preserved on a magnificent stela, or carved block, of diorite (inset). The code spells out edicts covering a wide range of legal matters. For example, the detail highlighted here reads: "If a free man has accused another free man and has brought a charge of murder against him but has not proved it, his accuser shall be put to death."

A sculpture depicting King Hammurabi decorates the top of the seven-foot-tall stela containing his epochal law code, which was written some-time after 1800 BC.

		a
		i
		â
		ou
		ou
		b
		p
		fg
		m
		n
		r
		h
		h
		kh
		kh
		s
		s
		ch
		k
		k
		g
		t
		tj
		d
		dj

The three hieroglyphic signs to the right spell the word meaning "eternity" in ancient Egyptian. The word appears here as a detail from a wall painting in the tomb of Queen Nefertari, wife of King Ramses II, who ruled in the thirteenth century BC.

READING EGYPTIAN

When the Egyptians first started to write, sometime around 3300 BC, their hieroglyphic signs may have stood for complete words or concepts, as did the pictographs of the Sumerians. The three birds in the left column of the chart probably meant what they look like: "vulture," "quail chick," and "owl."

But very shortly a number of the hieroglyphs took on phonetic values; the twenty-five signs shown here represented the spoken language's fundamental sounds. The owl stood for a sound rendered in English as "m"; the vulture for the sound of "a"; the stylized picture of a leg for the consonant "b"; and so on, as indicated in the chart's third column.

At the same time, a number of other hieroglyphs began to represent clusters of sounds. A picture of a bee, for example, indicated a syllable that was pronounced "bit." However, some hieroglyphs had pictographic meanings, denoting entire words. A sentence written in Egyptian could be baffling — a mix of phonetic symbols with what linguists call ideograms. This system became more ornate about 2900 BC, when scribes devised the script called hieratic *(second column in chart)*, in which the hieroglyphic signs were simplified and many were joined, as in modern cursive handwriting.

The hieratic script on the right side of the section of papyrus above poses questions about the geometry of the triangles on the left. The papyrus is part of the largest Egyptian mathematical textbook ever discovered, and it reveals much about how Egyptian engineers calculated the proportions of pyramids and other structures. Written around 1650 BC, the entire papyrus was originally a single roll about eighteen feet long by thirteen inches high.

The hieroglyphs above this figure of a scribe boast of his high standing in the community.

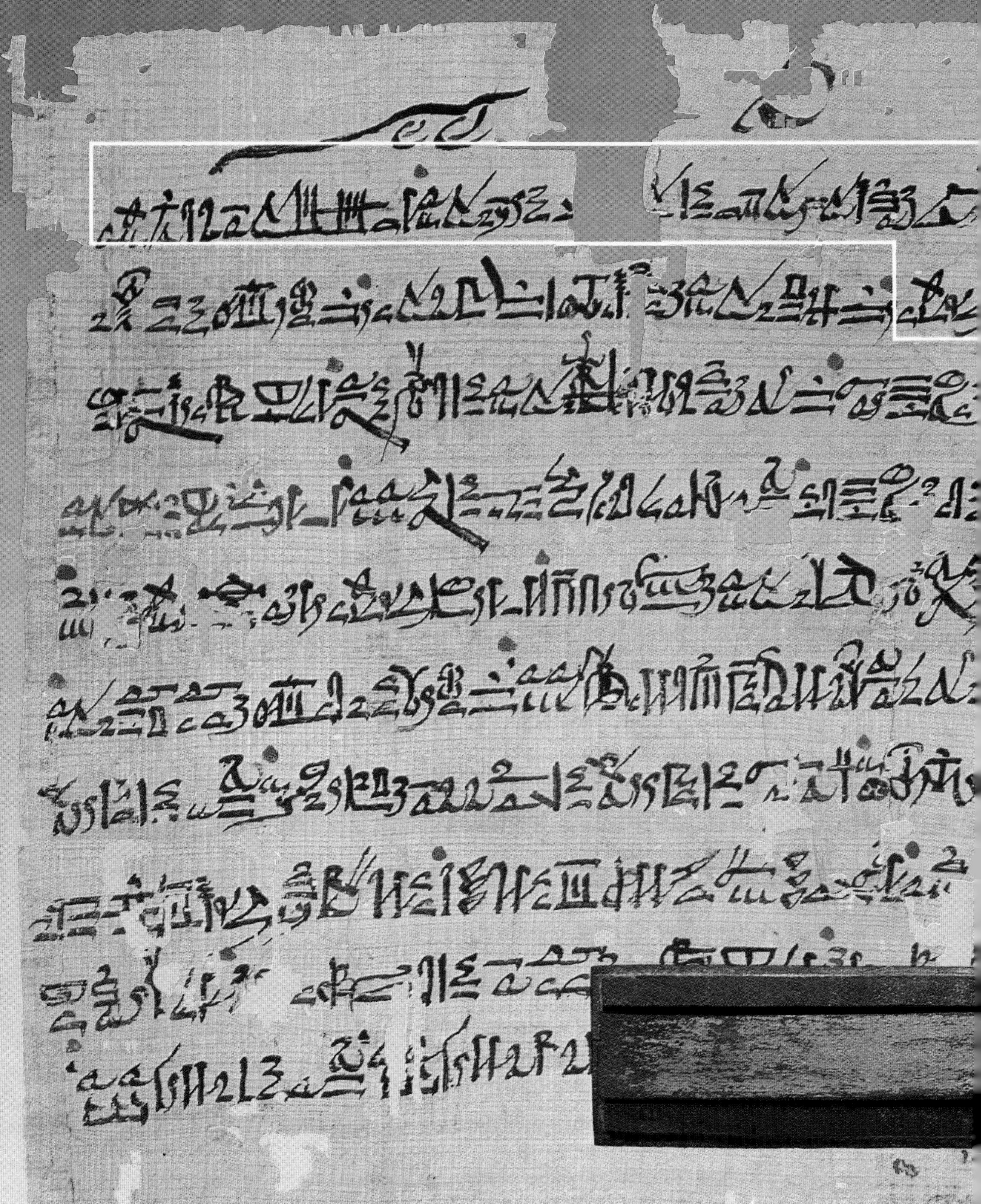

The flowing hieratic script came into wide use after the Egyptians had learned to make a paper-like writing material from the papyrus reed that flourished along the Nile. Egypt's dry climate gave the papyrus long life: The example at left is as legible as it was when written some 3,300 years ago. It tells a pharaoh's story of a battle against some rebellious subjects. The first line reads: "I woke up for the fighting, recovering consciousness and realizing that it was a fighting of the guard. If I had time to take my arms in hand, I could have beaten off the rebels."

An Egyptian scribe's wooden penholder contains the materials for writing on papyrus: a selection of reed pens and two ink pots, one for black ink and the other for the red used in highlighting the beginnings of sections of text.

The beautiful paintings that adorned the walls of many Egyptian tombs were usually accompanied by hieroglyphic texts. These texts served, in effect, as captions, identifying the individuals who were pictured and spelling out their worldly accomplishments. The highlighted hieroglyphics in the tomb chamber at right indicate that it was the resting place of Sen-nefer, a mayor of Thebes in the fifteenth century BC, and that the man and woman painted on the column were Sen-nefer and his wife. The first vertical line of the highlighted text says that the wife was a "singer of Amun"; that is, she helped the priests worship Egypt's leading deity. Another section of the text, starting with the fourth line from the left, names Sen-nefer; it lauds him as a "great confidant" of the pharaoh and as a "director of the priests of Amun."

Hieroglyphics indicate that the noble figure carved in the stela below was Prince Netcher-aperaf, a high-ranking member of the court of an early pharaoh named Sneferu. The prince was not only a priest and a royal scribe, the hieroglyphics report, but also a royal judge and a "director of missions" — presumably a post concerned with foreign affairs.

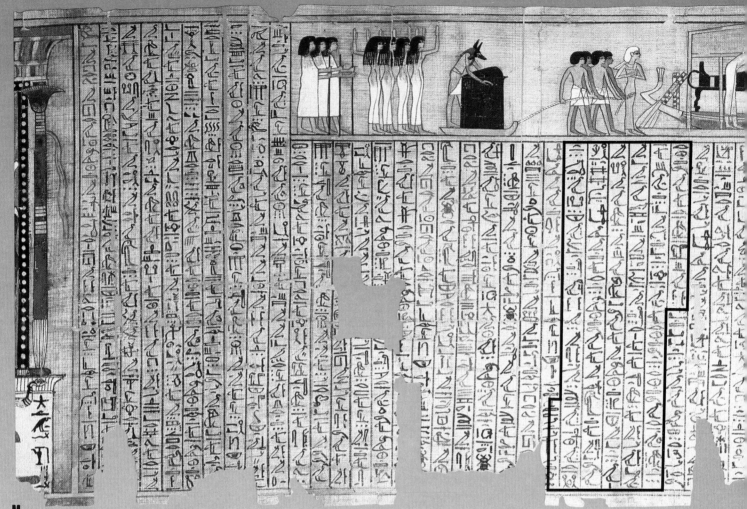

Many of the papyruses found in Egyptian tombs contain portions of a religious work known as the Book of the Dead. The Egyptians placed selections of the book's spells or prayers with a body, in the belief that the text would help speed the deceased toward a blissful afterlife.

The highlighted section of the long scroll above is a copy of spell number seventy-two (there are nearly 200 in all). It consists of a plea from the deceased that the gods will allow him to emerge from the tomb and see daylight again. The text begins: "Hail to you, who are perfect of soul, you owners of truth, who exist for all eternity! Open to me, for I am a spirit in my own shape."

Highlighted on the funeral papyrus at right is another spell from the Book of the Dead, this one meant to ensure that the heart of the deceased — the locus of individuality — would remain with the dead person in the next life. "My heart belongs to me in the house of the hearts," the passage begins, "and in me it rests." The scribe who copied out this spell made a number of errors, endowing the deceased at one point with two hearts.

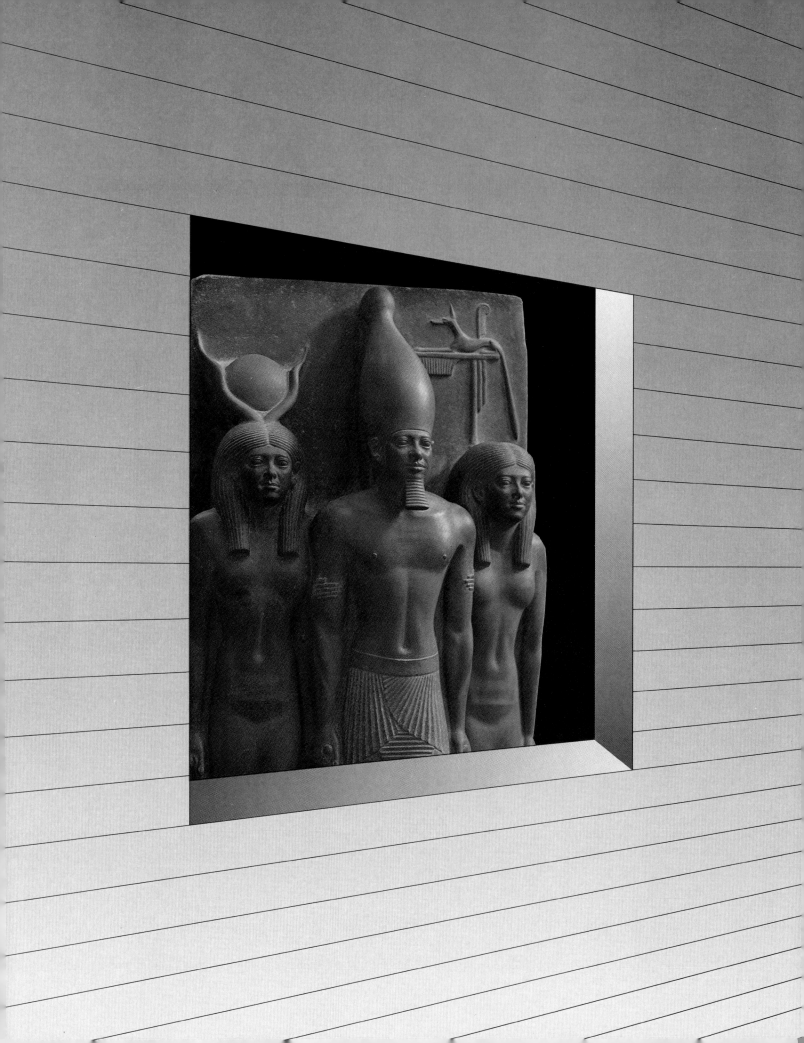

THE WAY OF THE PHARAOHS

Long before the first pharaohs raised their prodigious edifices along the Nile, signaling the emergence of the world's second great civilization, the river was a source of sustenance for small bands of hunter-gatherers. Fish and fowl abounded there; antelope frequented the shallows; and wild barley took root in the rich layer of silt deposited during the river's annual flood. The prehistoric peoples of the Nile harvested this bounty with stone blades and arrowheads. And when the cresting river threatened to inundate their camps, they simply withdrew into the nearby desert, biding their time until the waters receded.

This primitive, hand-to-mouth existence prevailed along the Nile until around 5200 BC — or some 2,000 years after the inhabitants of Mesopotamia had begun to work the soil. But slowly over the succeeding centuries, a fresh influx of settlers versed in the rudiments of agriculture changed the face of the Nile River valley. Some of these newcomers drifted in from the Fertile Crescent — that arc of arable land stretching from Mesopotamia to Palestine — bringing with them livestock and domestic strains of wheat and barley. In time, through migration and trade, a number of practices that had been fostered in Mesopotamia would find their way to Egypt, including the use of wheeled vehicles and elements of the Sumerian system of writing. Yet the most important link between the two cultures was the process of irrigation. Not long after the people of Sumer learned to raise dikes and dig canals, the inhabitants of the Nile Valley began to divert the river's floodwaters. As in Mesopotamia, that effort yielded two things crucial to the development of civilization: an agricultural surplus and a spirit of collective discipline.

The yearly flood that nurtured the crops of the Egyptians originated in equatorial Africa, where the 4,132-mile-long Nile arose. Beginning in late spring, monsoon winds sweeping from the Indian Ocean dumped torrential rains on the highlands of East Africa, feeding the tributary known as the Blue Nile. That swollen branch roiled northward through mountain gorges, tracts of marshland, and fetid jungles before merging with the White Nile near present-day Khartoum. Below the confluence lay a forbidding series of six cataracts. The northernmost — or First Cataract — marked the geographic boundary of Egypt.

Soon after the summer solstice, the flood surge reached the Nile Valley, a 500-mile-long cleft in the Sahara extending from the First Cataract north to the marshlands of the Nile Delta. Fortunately for the settlers of this fertile corridor — known as Upper Egypt — natural moundlike levees had built up along the Nile as its heavier deposits accumulated over the centuries. Sheltered from all but the most severe floods, villagers waited out the deluge in their mud huts atop these so-called tortoise backs — venturing abroad now and then in sturdy papyrus rafts to fish the muddy waters or to barter with neighboring villages. Later, as the Nile receded, the floodwaters were trapped in the natural depressions that flanked the tortoise backs. Now the peasants labored together to plant grain and to exploit those reservoirs for their seedlings, hauling the water in buckets to nearby plots or channeling it along shallow ditches.

The urge to expand these irrigation projects up and down the banks of the Nile promoted communal links all along the river. In time, groups of rural settlements were organized into provinces, or nomes, governed by chieftains, called nomarchs. With few forbidding civic or geographic barriers to overcome, the nomes of Upper Egypt were soon consolidated; the process began around 3500 BC, and within a century or two a single ruler held dominion over the region.

To the north, however, in the wetland of the Delta, a different set of conditions prevailed. There, most settlements were isolated year round on sandy mounds above the marsh. Until large portions of the swamp were reclaimed by the pharaohs, this region, known as Lower Egypt, was a land of more peril than productivity: Herders tended cattle in swampy pastures where crocodiles lay in wait for the stray calf, while hunters took to the meandering watercourses armed with spears against the hippopotamus — a volatile beast capable of crushing a man between its jaws. This way of life reinforced the age-old virtues of bravery and resourcefulness yet did little to sharpen political instincts.

Naturally enough, the unification of Upper and Lower Egypt was sparked not among the communities of the Delta but in the more cohesive Nile Valley. Just who was responsible for bringing the two regions together remains unresolved. Egyptian tradition tells of a god-king named Menes, a figure whose celebrated feats may in fact represent the accomplishments of a succession of ambitious overlords between 3200 and 3000 BC — among them the shadowy kings identified as Narmer and Aha on ancient carvings. In any event, Menes was memorialized as a leader of Upper Egypt who, through military conquest and political machinations, extended his domain to Lower Egypt. To commemorate his triumph, it was said, he built the white-walled capital of Memphis on land reclaimed from the Nile near the strategic point where the river branches out to form the Delta.

The proud new state consolidated by the mysterious Menes would grow to maturity in relative isolation. Bordered by desert expanses to the east and west, by cataracts to the south, and by a vast sea to the north, Egypt would suffer few hostile incursions in the centuries to come. And while Egyptian merchants pursued foreign trade and Egyptian soldiers made occasional forays across the borders, there was little need for campaigns of conquest: The river itself rendered ample tribute to the people. Unlike the erratic Euphrates in Sumer, the Nile rose and fell with a regularity that encouraged agricultural planning and building projects while instilling in the culture a sense of harmony. As the river counted out the

From the beginning, the fertile land along the Nile was divided naturally into two regions: Upper Egypt, the narrow river valley extending northward from the First Cataract; and Lower Egypt, the marsh country of the Nile Delta. By 3000 BC, these regions were united under one king, who made his capital at Memphis, near the junction of Upper and Lower Egypt; in time, vast funeral complexes grew up at nearby Saqqara and Giza to house the remains of the pharaohs and their courtiers. Elsewhere along the Nile, important villages developed into cities that would come to rival Memphis for supremacy — among them Thebes and Heliopolis, home of the prestigious sun cult.

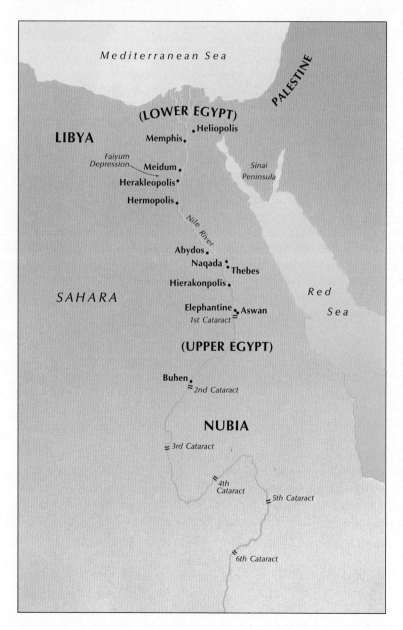

Even as they learned to harness the Nile's floodwaters, the Egyptians were taking to the river in sailing craft. This relief, which was carved around 2400, shows a pair of vessels with the distinctive two-legged mast devised by Egyptian shipwrights to distribute the weight of mast and sail over the hull of the boat. When the wind failed and rowing became necessary, the boat's crew un-stepped the mast with the aid of ropes that the sailors had carried aboard around their necks *(center)* or looped over one of the large steering paddles *(left)*.

years and centuries in flawless cadence, that culture would produce a system of writing distinguished by graceful, natural symbols; a phalanx of fearsome gods and a temple-focused government; and an artistic, architectural, and engineering genius that expressed itself in astonishing monuments.

The political consolidation of Egypt around 3000 BC marked the rise of the first dynasty of pharaohs. Twenty-nine such dynasties would follow — with shifts in lineage occasioned by the absence of heirs or by violent upheaval — before Egypt fell subject to the Greeks under Alexander. The word *pharaoh* means simply "great house," and one of the missions of the first pharaohs was to establish their spiritual supremacy over all the other influential houses in the land.

Since early times, the local chieftains of Egypt had laid claim to mystical powers. Each important village had its patron deity, and the noble who controlled the area took up residence near the temple of the god, where he could invoke his divine patron's blessing. Often the god was represented as an animal, a reflection of the awe with which the early Nile dwellers regarded the creatures that shared their fertile homeland. Thus the ruler of Naqada in Upper Egypt derived his authority from the truculent god Seth, pictured as a fierce, long-snouted beast, and the chieftain of nearby Nekhen secured strength and cunning from the falcon-god Horus. In time, myths associated with these local deities were combined to form a compelling legend that told of a bitter power struggle and celebrated the emergence of a god-king for all Egypt.

According to one popular version of this legend, Horus was the son of Osiris, a god of nature whose power was manifest in the ebb and flood of the Nile. Osiris himself had once ruled Egypt, aided by his wife and sister, Isis, before he was brought down by his murderously jealous brother Seth, who dismembered Osiris and scattered his parts over the land. The faithful Isis went about collecting the pieces and patched them back together, thus resurrecting Osiris, who retired from his earthly responsibilities to become lord of the afterworld.

Horus was left to contend with his uncle, Seth, for dominion over Egypt. Ultimately, the two met in epic combat; although Horus lost an eye, he succeeded in castrating Seth, and in a subsequent hearing, the earth god, Geb, declared Horus the victor and pronounced him King of Egypt. With the emergence of the pharaohs, the message of the legend was unmistakable: There would be a single ruler for Egypt, and he would be the incarnation of the greatest of Egypt's gods. Each pharaoh was the human form of

Horus. Upon his death, he became one with Osiris and reigned supreme in the next life, while his heir ruled on earth as the new incarnation of the great falcon-god.

The tale of primal conflict and restitution not only provided a religious rationale for the power wielded by the pharaoh but also helped fuel a royal obsession with death and mortuary rituals. A great imperative was defined by the reconstruction of the dismembered Osiris: The body of the god-king had to be preserved intact in order for him to attain immortality. The belief that fulfillment in the afterlife depended on the preservation of the body was shared by all Egyptians. Villagers buried their dead in the sand—which helped to preserve the remains—along with food and drink meant to nourish the deceased on the journey to the next world. But sustaining the dead body of the pharaoh was a matter of special urgency, for the god-king was part of the cosmic order.

To shield their remains throughout eternity, the pharaohs of the First Dynasty built sturdy tombs in Upper Egypt at Abydos, a town that was destined to become the center of the Osiris cult. Abydos was nearly 300 miles south of the palace at Memphis, but a journey of such a distance could be easily accomplished on Egypt's great river highway. Already, sizable boats made of reeds, with upswept prows and square linen sails, were plying the Nile alongside the rafts of peasants and peddlers. This kind of sailing vessel, propelled by the prevailing northerly wind that swept from the Mediterranean, may well have been used to ferry the pharaoh's body to its destination, affording thousands of his former subjects the opportunity to pause in their labors along the banks of the river and pay homage to their deceased ruler.

Hunters in a papyrus skiff *(left)* take aim at a hippopotamus lurking below the surface beside a crocodile; one harpoon thrust has already hit home, snagging the quarry with a detachable barb held on a line. Egyptians celebrated many animals in myths and portrayed them in exquisite miniatures that served as charms. The hedgehog *(far left)*, though sometimes hunted and eaten, was honored for its ability to retreat into deathlike hibernation each winter and revive with the spring; the crocodile was feared and exalted as the embodiment of the god Sobek; and the hippopotamus, in statuette form, accompanied people to the grave, perhaps to symbolize the taming of the forces of evil by the human spirit.

The tomb that awaited the pharaoh at Abydos was a substantial structure known as a mastaba. Meant to endure forever, it was built of sun-baked mud bricks, with a flat roof and sloping sides. Inside were compartments stocked with an array of offerings—food, furniture, tools, and weapons—to fortify the dead king in the hereafter. Beneath the structure was a shaft that led to an underground chamber, hewn from rock and lined with brick. There the pharaoh's body would rest.

Surrounding the mastabas at Abydos were burial pits for the king's faithful retainers, including concubines, court dwarfs, and even pet dogs. All were expected to accompany the king into the afterworld. Indeed, there is some evidence that as many as 580 members of the court of King Djer, who ruled Egypt around 2900, were put to death so

that they might carry on in his service. But the Egyptians were by no means a bloodthirsty people, and in time the sacrifices ceased and burial near the pharaoh was reserved for royal kinfolk and valued subjects.

The introduction of the mastaba gave impetus to a new craft at court—embalming. Separated from the drying sands by walls of brick, a corpse quickly decayed. The first measure taken in response to this problem was cosmetic: Swathing the body in linen bandages soaked in resin preserved the form of the body even as the flesh moldered within. This simple process yielded some impressive results. The linen-wrapped vestige of an arm, believed to be that of King Djer himself, was uncovered in a plundered mastaba at Abydos nearly 5,000 years after the pharaoh had been interred. But the royal embalmers were not long content with preserving appearances. By the beginning of the Fourth Dynasty, around 2600 BC, they were taking the first step toward true mummification. They removed the dead pharaoh's internal organs through an incision in the abdomen and placed them in a so-called canopic jar, a vessel filled with a salty solution known as natron. The body cavity was then dried and packed with resin-soaked linen before the exterior was prepared — attentions that might include highlighting the face with green paint or decking out the shrouded corpse in jewelry and elegant robes.

Not long after King Djer went to his grave with a legion of servants, the royal burial site was shifted from Abydos to Saqqara, much closer to Memphis. Over the years, the mastabas there grew more imposing — up to seventeen feet high, with as many as seventy chambers. Some of the structures featured a room from which the spirit of the deceased, represented by a statue, could gaze through a slot into an adjoining chamber to consider new supplies brought by priests. (As practical as they were superstitious, the priests often consumed the offerings before the food or drink had time to spoil.) Below ground, and leading horizontally to the sarcophagus chamber, was a large hall that was filled with rubble immediately after the burial to deter tomb robbers, who had already become a bane.

With the reign of the Third Dynasty's King Djoser, around 2650, the royal burial place underwent a radical transformation. By this time, the power of the pharaoh was absolute, and all Egyptians — from the proudest of nomarchs to the lowliest of slaves — were subject to his dictates. As if to proclaim his exalted status, Djoser commissioned at Saqqara the world's first great stone structure — an eternal house that would reach for the heavens.

Timber was scarce in Egypt, but stone was plentiful. The Aswan area, 450 miles south of Saqqara near the First Cataract, yielded granite, basalt, and quartz; the hills of Tura, on the east bank, across from Saqqara, afforded a fine, white limestone. Peasants were conscripted in droves to labor for the king, and they soon mastered the art of working the quarries and transporting huge blocks overland on rollers or sleds and along the Nile by barge. In erecting his tomb, King Djoser also had the benefit of the services of a versatile genius named Imhotep. Besides being the high priest of an increasingly influential sun cult centered at the temple of Heliopolis, Imhotep was the pharaoh's vizier, or chief counselor, and an accomplished sculptor. Yet his supreme achievement was as Djoser's architect.

The tomb Imhotep designed for Djoser took the mastaba form to new heights. Assembling hundreds of thousands of limestone blocks, Imhotep in effect built six mastabas of diminishing size, one on the other. The result was a ziggurat-like tower known as the Step Pyramid, a name that suggests its spiritual function. As a sacred text expressed it: "A staircase to heaven is laid for him [the king] so that he may mount up to heaven thereby." Dominating the horizon at Saqqara, Djoser's monument rose 204 feet and measured 413 feet by 344 feet at its base. A wide central shaft led underground from the base of the pyramid to the king's granite burial chamber, which was flanked by galleries crammed with funerary offerings held in more than 40,000 stone vases.

This carved slate commemorates the exploits of King Narmer *(center)*, who came to power in the Nile Valley around the year 3100 and played an important part in the unification of Egypt. Backed by his sandal bearer and wearing the elongated crown of Upper Egypt, Narmer raises his club to strike an enemy; the falcon-god Horus *(upper right)* — patron of Narmer and of all future pharaohs — holds a victim tethered amid tall strands of papyrus, emblematic of marshy Lower Egypt.

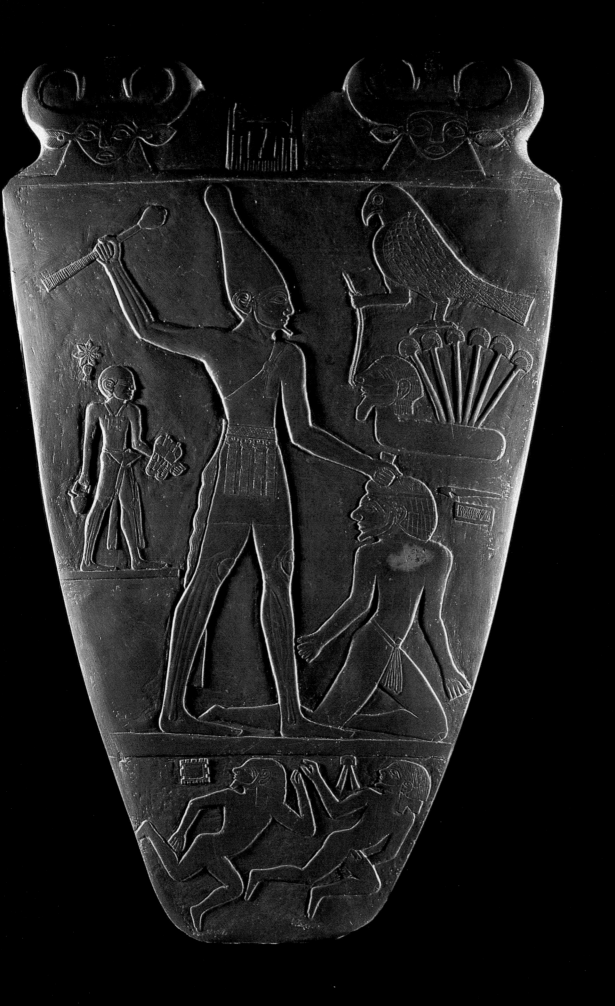

King Djoser's six-step pyramid at Saqqara stood amid a complex of structures designed to glorify the pharaoh in the afterlife. Only priests were permitted within this walled necropolis, some of whose buildings were mere façades: The long gallery at the west side of the compound *(background)* was filled with rubble that covered a fabulous cache of royal treasures. The king's mortuary temple extended northward from the base of the pyramid; within that sanctuary, priests regularly burned incense and made offerings of food and drink as a statue of Djoser looked on. The area south of the pyramid was reserved for the pharaoh's *sed* festival, a jubilee celebrated by the king in death as in life. The two stones shaped like the letter *B* in the central courtyard marked a course run by the pharaoh's spirit during this ritual. The shrines aligned nearby *(detail, left)* sheltered the various local gods of Egypt; their attendance at the jubilee signified the allegiance of each province and its patron deity to the supreme lord of the land.

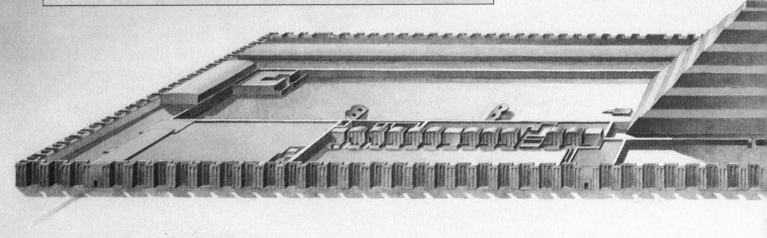

Djoser's pyramid was the center of a cluster of mortuary buildings, temples, and courts, one of which was equipped with a dais so that the dead king's spirit could take part in a kind of royal jubilee known as the *sed,* a ritual reenactment of his inauguration. Around the entire pyramid complex was a massive stone wall, thirty-three feet high and about a mile long. Perhaps to frustrate intruders, the wall had thirteen false portals and one real entryway, all of them identical to the eye.

Within fifty years, the design of pyramids changed. Indeed, the transition appears to have come within the reign of a single pharaoh: Sneferu, the first king of the Fourth Dynasty. At Meidum, south of Memphis, an eight-step pyramid was constructed, either by Sneferu or by his immediate predecessor. Then, at Sneferu's behest, the steps were filled in with rubble and the entire structure was encased in Turan limestone to give it the smooth sides of a true pyramid.

Significantly, this architectural development coincided with the emergence of the sun god, Re, as the country's dominant deity. Egypt was a land where the blazing power of the sun was felt year round, and where the rays dried the ground after the Nile's annual flood, ushering in the season of growth. The pharaohs were eager to identify themselves with such mystic power. Thus the pyramid was conceived as a sunburst in stone, its sides reproducing the slant of the sun's rays as they angled toward the earth through a break in the clouds. "May heaven strengthen the sun's rays for you," read one pyramid inscription addressed to the pharaoh, "so that you may ascend to heaven as the eye of Re." To honor Re, the temples adjoining the pyramids would be oriented to the east, with their entrances facing the rising sun.

The masterworks that emerged along the Nile in response to such impulses testified

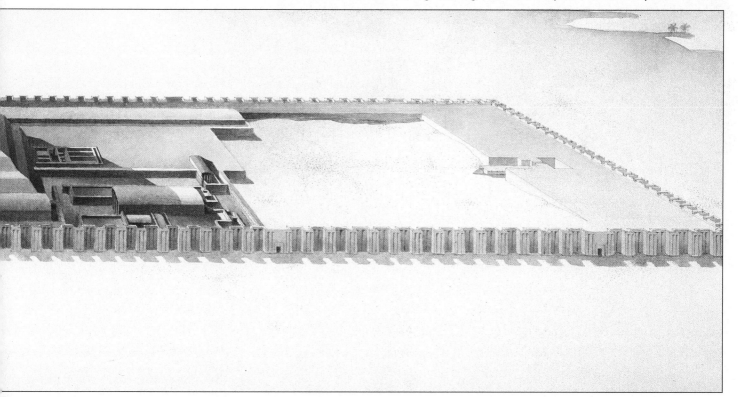

to the pharaoh's divine aspirations and the extraordinary authority he exercised. The shape of the pyramid reflected the organizing principle of Egyptian society: The pharaoh stood at the apex, and a coterie of officials, priests, and scribes near the top were supported in their lofty endeavors by the peasant masses laboring below.

The pharaoh was lord of the land in the most literal sense. Though priests and officials might run prosperous estates, their rights to the land and all it produced were derived from the king, who was master of the fields and laid claim to a portion of their bounty. He controlled the Nile through the magical powers of his godliness and through more practical devices, such as the levees and canals he authorized. He was the commander of all Egyptians: Every person, from fieldhand to royal kinsman, was subject to the pharaoh's summons for whatever duties the god-king might choose to assign. He was the source of all justice, and in the absence of a legal code or a body of precedent, his word became law. He was the dispenser of wealth and the regulator of trade. In short, as proclaimed in an inscription in the tomb of a nomarch named Ameny, the pharaoh was the "superintendent of all things which heaven gives and the earth produces."

As a practical matter, it was necessary for the king to delegate most of his duties. Thus, in one of the most centralized of states ever known evolved one of humanity's more imposing bureaucracies.

At the top of the administrative system stood the vizier, an official with a host of titles and at least thirty major functions. He managed the royal residence; he supervised all public works; he directed military forays and acted as the national chief of police; he commissioned a vast array of royal artisans; he dispensed justice by presiding over the high court; he oversaw the royal farms and granaries, monitoring the distribution of food to the many laborers and officials who depended on the pharaoh for sustenance; and most important of all, he was responsible for the collection of taxes.

Ranking just below the vizier was the chancellor, who was followed in order of authority by the nomarchs, or provincial governors. Periodically, nomarchs would form alliances and challenge the sovereignty of the pharaoh. But by and large, they were faithful officers who saw themselves as the local representatives of the king's righteousness. "All the works of the king came into my hand," boasted one nomarch. "There was not the daughter of a poor man that I wronged, nor a widow that I oppressed. There was not a farmer that I chastised, not a herdsman that I drove away. There was not a pauper around me, there was not a hungry man of my time."

Such was the ideal of Egyptian government. In practice, however, the main concern of the authorities was not to dispense goodness and mercy but to exact services and levy taxes. The tax system was elaborate. Property, according to an official decree, was assessed for its "canals, lakes, wells, waterways, and trees." The herder was taxed for his cattle, the artisan for his wares. But the major source of revenue in the heavily agrarian economy was, of course, Egypt's crops.

For the purpose of determining taxes, the land was divided into tracts: those that regularly received the blessings of the Nile's annual floods, those that sometimes did, and those that seldom or never did. Every year, taxes were calculated according to the flood stage at various locations along the river, beginning at the island of Elephantine near the First Cataract. There, from the time of Egypt's First Dynasty, the height of the flood was measured — originally by a simple set of markings on the Nile's rocky banks

An Egyptian scribe sits in a cross-legged position — the customary posture for writing — and uses his taut kilt as a support for the papyrus scroll that he grips in his left hand. This painted limestone statue, which was carved around 2400 BC, is believed to represent a provincial governor of the Fifth Dynasty: High Egyptian officials were schooled as scribes, and they took pride in their mastery of the written word.

and later on by a nilometer, a calibrated stairway that descended into the river. Thus, for example, a flood level of twenty-six feet meant a "good Nile." Based on this measurement, the annual tax rates were set, crop quotas were assigned, seed was dispensed from the royal stores to those who required it, and cattle were loaned for plowing from the royal herds. When the harvest was in, the vizier's collectors, accompanied by police carrying sticks to enforce compliance, spread like locusts across the land.

The surrendering of tax grain did not signal even a brief respite for the hard-worked peasantry. During the time of Inundation, which began in July and culminated around September, they could be conscripted into the army of the pharaoh's pyramid builders. Then as the Nile receded, a period known to the Egyptians as the Emergence, they took to the fields, channeling the waters, tilling the soil with wooden plows, and sowing barley, emmer, and flax. In the last of Egypt's three seasons — the Drought, which began in February — they brought in the harvest, threshed grain under the hoofs of donkeys or cattle, and when the tax collectors had taken their share of the yield, used what remained to bake the bread and brew the beer that were the staples of their diet.

The surplus levied from the peasants each year went to support not only the pharaoh and his household but also the households of government officials and others favored with the king's patronage. Such wealthy families enjoyed opulent lifestyles. Their spacious homes, built around open courtyards, were furnished with elegant chairs with comfortable seats of linen cord, beds with headrests, and game boards inlaid with faience and ivory. The household staffs were large and included bakers, brewers, gardeners, musicians, and handmaidens. Some of these domestics were native-born servants; others might be slaves captured by Egyptian troops during forays into such hostile lands as Syria and Nubia. Those who waited on guests at table wore little more than a breechcloth. In contrast, those being served were dressed in white linen garments and wore tightly braided black wigs, and collars of brightly colored beads that jewelers strung with spangles of gold or silver. Feasts were boisterous affairs; while picking from platters heaped high with bread, figs, and dates, the celebrants were serenaded by harpists. The main dish was usually a hand-fed goose, roasted on a spit over embers and then brushed with a straw whisk to clean off the soot. Beer and wine were consumed freely, both having been fermented on the premises.

All aspects of social and economic life, from the routine of the great households to the output of the peasantry, were subject to meticulous record keeping. As in Sumer, this need prompted the development of writing as a craft. In its written language as in its agricultural practices, Egypt was doubtless influenced by the pioneering achievements of Mesopotamian culture. But — as they did with almost everything they borrowed — the Egyptians soon placed their own, conservative stamp on the written form. While the Sumerians moved fairly rapidly from pictographs to wedge-shaped cuneiform characters that formed syllables and words, the Egyptians continued to rely on exquisite characters representing animals, objects, places, people — and parts thereof. Some of these symbols stood for things or ideas; others stood for sounds. Elegant but cumbersome to use, such formal hieroglyphs served throughout the history of dynastic Egypt for monument inscriptions. But a more condensed and cursive style, called hieratic, was soon adopted for everyday notations, easing the task of the scribes.

The spread of Egyptian writing was greatly aided by a bounty of the Nile: the tall papyrus reed, which grew in abundance along the banks of the river and in the Delta's marshes. Flat strips of the reed's pith were laid down in two layers, one perpendicular

The ibis-headed deity Thoth *(left)* demonstrates the art of writing, a skill he was said to have imparted to the Egyptians at the dawn of time. In applying their talent, Egyptian scribes relied on the papyrus plant: As early as 3100, papyrus reeds were being harvested along the Nile *(far left)*. These reeds were then stretched out in layers on a frame and pounded together to produce a parchmentlike writing surface *(top)*.

to the other; when moistened, pounded smooth, and dried, this mat yielded a writing surface much like that of paper. Lightweight, portable, easy to store, and fairly durable, papyrus was far more convenient than the clay tablets of the Sumerians. An Egyptian monopoly, it would long be one of the country's primary exports.

At first, writing was used largely to list the names of kings and record the significant events of their reigns. But with the burgeoning of the bureaucracy, literate men became vital to the conduct of government. "It is to writings that you must set your mind," one official told his son. To satisfy such a parental injunction, the child had to enroll in a scribal school. There he would labor from dawn to dusk for a dozen or more years, using his palette and black ink, his rush brushes, and his erasing stone to perfect his knowledge of some 700 signs. He mastered those intricate symbols by practicing

Workmen wield adzes to shape and smooth the hull of a boat in this relief from the mastaba of a nobleman named Ti, who was buried at Saqqara around 2350 BC. In exchange for loyalty to the pharaoh, important officials like Ti were granted royal permission to operate large estates, where they commanded the efforts of peasants, domestics, scribes, and even shipwrights. The labors of such servants were then depicted on the walls of the landholder's tomb as a means of retaining their services in the netherworld.

endlessly on drearily familiar formulas — a warehouse inventory, perhaps, or the salutation to a letter: "May you prosper, may you live, may I see you again in safety and fold you in my embrace."

Discipline in the schools took its tenor from the maxim "A boy's ears are on his back." Whippings were frequent. Yet the prize was worth the pain, for being a scribe was one of the few avenues to advancement in this rigidly stratified society. During the reign of Ammenemes III, in the fourteenth century BC, a royal scribe who bore the same name as the pharaoh rose to become the king's vizier and was rewarded with his own mortuary temple. Later generations would worship him for his wisdom.

For the most part, the men who taught the scribes their craft were priests. Indeed, in Egypt as in other great civilizations, the priesthood was a fountainhead of scholarship and science. The sun and the stars were filled with religious significance for the Egyptians, and so the priests became adept at astronomy. They learned to calculate the moment at which the rays of the rising or setting sun would strike the tip of any pyramid and give off the blinding glint that brought a peak of excitement to sacred ceremonies. And they observed that the brightest of stars, Sirius, rose in the east just ahead of the sun once a year (on July 19 by the modern calendar) and that this event foretold within a few days the arrival of the Nile's annual flood. The day on which Sirius rose with the sun became the first day of the Egyptian year, which consisted of twelve months, each with thirty days. Five additional days were set aside for festivals commemorating the birthdays of Osiris, Horus, Isis, and even the infamous Seth and his wife Nephythys.

For all the priests' learned activities, however, the function of their office was not to interpret nature but to celebrate its miraculous powers. The Egyptian pantheon, with its multitude of gods portrayed as animals, would later bewilder foreigners. "What monsters are revered by demented Egypt?" asked the Roman satirist Juvenal. "One part worships the crocodile. Another goes in awe of the ibis, which feeds on serpents. Elsewhere, there shines the golden effigy of the long-tailed monkey."

Yet there was nothing demented about it. To the earliest Egyptians, the power of the gods was plainly visible in the natural world — in the Nile itself, a miraculous wellspring of life amid the desert wastes, and in all of the river's denizens: the beasts that grazed on its floodplain, the creatures that swam in its waters or slithered along its banks, the birds that rose from its shallows to circle the sky above. It was entirely fitting that immortal beings should reveal themselves in these ceaseless wonders — that Horus should appear as a falcon, the god Khnum as a ram, the god Thoth as an ibis, the goddess Hathor as a cow, the god Sobek as a crocodile. What the Egyptians worshipped was not the animal itself but the divine spirit that animated it, a pliant force that could take many forms. Thus the goddess Taweret, thought to protect mothers from evil forces during childbirth, was represented by a beast with the head of a hippopotamus, the back and tail of a crocodile, the claws of a lion and the breasts of a woman. As civilization developed, the deities were imagined in more human terms; Horus, for instance, was pictured with the head of a falcon but the body of a man.

The Egyptians saw gods in the heavens as well. The rising sun was the god Re embarking on a boat that would carry him to the western horizon. There he would transfer to a nighttime vessel and sail through the afterworld until he reached the dawn once more. Even

In this tomb relief, sculptors finish a statue with hammer and chisel. Sculptors were among the most richly rewarded of Egyptian artisans because their works conferred immortality by providing an eternal refuge for the *ka*, or life force, of the person represented.

the Egyptians' story of the Creation was based on an event they witnessed in the world around them. During severe floods, the huge earthen mounds known as tortoise backs might be swallowed up by the Nile, forcing those who lived there to take refuge at the fringe of the desert. Those humps were of course the first glistening islands that emerged as the flood receded. To the Egyptians, such mounds represented an ascendance of the replenished land. So it had been during the Creation, when the primeval mound of the universe rose from the waters of Chaos.

The myth varied in its details from place to place, and even the identity of the Creator was open to argument. At various times, the priests of Memphis, Heliopolis, Hermopolis, and Thebes each claimed that their city was the site of the Creation, and each ascribed the feat to its local god. But the rivalries made little difference. What mattered was that, annually, Egyptians beheld a reenactment of the miracle of Creation.

Of the religions that flourished with the world's first civilizations, that of the Egyptians was perhaps the most benevolent, the most flexible, and the most hospitable. Lacking a book of sacred writ or a body of commandments, the Egyptians' religion nonetheless offered a unifying principle known as *maat*, personified by the goddess Maat. The concept has been translated as justice, truth, order, and righteousness. But maat offered more, for it represented the cosmic order that emerged at the time of the Creation. Thus, as explained by an early text, the Creator came from the primeval mound only "after he had put maat in the place of Chaos." As a god on earth, the pharaoh was responsible for administering maat according to his divine judgment; as the same text elaborated: "Heaven is satisfied and the earth rejoices when they hear that King Pepy II has put maat in the place of disorder."

The Egyptian pantheon always had room for a new god, and at one time or another as many as 2,000, including several of foreign origin, made up the divine coterie. Some gods, among them Osiris and Horus, were national deities. Yet the predynastic practice by which every province and every village worshipped its own god persisted under the pharaohs, and the influence of these deities would wax or wane according to shifts in political fortunes. Thus the god Ptah, patron of Memphis, was exalted as the Creator and as the sponsor of royalty by the early pharaohs who made their capital there. By the Fourth Dynasty, the center the Greeks would label Heliopolis, or "City of the Sun," was on the rise, and soon each pharaoh was proclaiming himself the son of Re (even while continuing as Horus, son of Osiris). Later, around the year 2000, after a prince from Thebes fought his way to the throne, the previously obscure god of the Thebans came to the fore. His name was Amun, an elusive god of air and light who might take the earthly form of a ram or a goose. Eventually he became one with Re, a union that yielded the wealthiest of all Egypt's gods. In time, no less than one-tenth of the land would be held in the name of Amun-Re, including 433 gardens, 40 workshops, 65 towns, 400,000 animals, and to work the property, some 90,000 people.

This vast cult and the many smaller ones that took root in Egypt owed their holdings to the largesse of pharaohs, royal kinfolk, and other wealthy individuals who sought to curry the favor of a particular god by supporting that god's priests. As a divine being himself, the pharaoh presided over all cults, and the peasants on the priestly estates were referred to as the king's laborers. But over the years, as dynasty succeeded dynasty, the cults gained power, permanence, and a degree of independence from the whims of any one pharaoh. Recognizing this, some kings endowed pious foundations of their own to ensure that respect would be paid to them through the ages.

Though priests often performed important secular tasks, as illustrated by the archi-

An Egyptian official contemplates his courtyard, a meticulously landscaped retreat of the sort that graced many a spacious villa maintained by the wealthy. Beside him, his wife holds in her hand a lotus blossom, freshly picked from the pool. The lotus, represented here in outline atop the portico's front columns, was revered by the Egyptians as a symbol of regeneration: It rose from the water each dawn to open its petals to the sun god Re.

tectural feats of Imhotep, their sacred duties set them apart from the rest of the population, and they bore marks of exclusivity. Throughout the land, circumcised priests shaved off all body hair, including eyebrows and lashes, and they conducted their rites cloaked in white garments and animal skins. Although the ceremonies varied from cult to cult, at least one ritual was common to nearly all.

With the approach of day, a small group of the cult's high-ranking priests prepared for their duties by purifying themselves in a sacred pool. Then, in solemn procession, they moved across an open court and into the temple, which was closed to the public. At dawn's first ray, the clay seals to the inner sanctuary were broken, and the doors opened to disclose the god's effigy. The highest priest entered and lay prostrate before the image. Upon arising, he uttered prayers and perfumed the air with incense. He removed the god's raiment, cleansed the effigy, clothed it in fresh apparel, and offered it food and drink. Only after he performed these services did the priest depart, resealing the doors and expunging his footprints as well as all other signs of his attendance.

The most important duties in the religious life of Egypt were carried out by the pharaoh himself. As high priest of the land, he presided over elaborate rituals that invoked the cooperation of the Nile and the fertility of the soil. Theoretically, he had exclusive control over the appointment of priests. In practice, though, pharaohs were

reluctant to interfere in the affairs of established cults; priestly office thus became largely hereditary, passing from father to son. But those who inherited lofty positions could appoint subalterns, and in time the priesthood became heavily layered.

At the top were the chief priests and the select few of their company who were permitted to enter the inner sanctums of the temples. At the next level was a whole host of trained specialists — astrologers, scribes, readers of sacred texts, and singers and musicians (making music for the god was one of the few priestly roles to which women could aspire). On the bottom level were the common clergy, who served in such capacities as bearers of incense burners or interpreters of dreams.

Only the highest priests worked full time at their religious jobs. The specialists and common clergy served on a part-time basis, living on the temple grounds and executing their holy functions one month out of every four. While on duty, they lived ascetically, washing themselves with great frequency and practicing celibacy. Once their rotation was over, they rejoined the lay population for the next three months.

Within the thick husk of Egyptian religion, with its layers of cults and attendants, lay an enduring kernel of beliefs concerning the next life. For his part, the pharaoh anticipated the moment when he would take his rightful place among the gods. As one inscription in a king's tomb pronounced: ''Pepy ascends to heaven. He embarks in the

Herders prod cattle along with sticks as scribes squatting on the porch of an estate take inventory of the herd. Looking on from the tall chair is the landlord, Meketre, a Theban who served as Egypt's chancellor around 2000 BC and in whose tomb this set of wooden figurines was discovered. Grazing land was scarce in Upper Egypt, and for part of the year herds like the one depicted would be driven hundreds of miles north to feed in the lush Delta; on their return, the cattle would be counted, and the headman — shown here facing Meketre — would have to answer to his master for any losses.

boat of Re." (To assist the pharaohs on that heavenly voyage, great funerary boats were placed near their tombs.) Lesser folk expected to dwell in a perpetual domain of their own, usually said to be somewhere below the western horizon, a realm free of all earthly afflictions — drought, disease, famine, or war.

The Egyptians conceived of life after death not as the survival of a single, coherent spirit but as a complex process involving various ghostly components of the self. Most remote was the *akh,* or "transfigured spirit," which was thought to leave the body after death to revolve eternally in the heavens as a circumpolar star. A less ethereal component, the dead person's *ba* — a word that translates inadequately as "soul" — was depicted as a human-headed bird; it could flit about at will, yet it always returned to the dead body, its perpetual roost. A third element, known as the *ka,* was tied even more closely to the body. This was the life force that provided the energy for the dead to perform such duties as the sowing and reaping of grain — chores that were as necessary in the next world as they had been on earth. The ka was the recipient of the gifts left by the living to sustain the dead, as evidenced by a typical offertory inscription: "A thousand loaves of bread and jars of beer, together with all good and pure things for the ka of the deceased."

In coping with the bodily needs of the departed, the Egyptians demonstrated remarkable ingenuity. Indeed, their whole approach to the afterlife, like their conception of the gods on earth, was an imaginative blend of the physical and the spiritual, the literal and the symbolic. They knew that they could never furnish enough food to sustain the dead through eternity, so they left scythes nearby for the deceased to wield, or they depicted a harvest scene on the tomb walls as a substitute. They were conscious that a prosperous landholder should not be expected to fend for himself in the next world, so they furnished him with figurines known as *ushebte,* or "answerers," who would heed the call of the deceased and reap his grain. They realized that even the most elaborate preparations could not protect the corpse against desecration or decay, so they placed a statue of the deceased in a separate chamber and vested it with the power to assume the vital functions of the body if necessary.

Even after burial, the dead remained very much alive to those they left behind; it was a common practice for relatives to seek the intercession of the deceased in earthly affairs. In a letter placed in a woman's tomb by her kin, the deceased was asked to resolve a quarrel between her two sons — one dead, the other living. In another such communication, a hapless widower remonstrated with his dead wife: "What harm have I done you that I should be the poor man that I am? Why have you set your heart on weighing me down, I who was always your faithful husband?"

For better or worse, the people of Egypt were beholden to the past, as embodied by the spirit of the departed. Therefore, it was only natural that the enduring symbols of

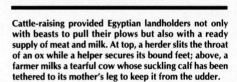

Cattle-raising provided Egyptian landholders not only with beasts to pull their plows but also with a ready supply of meat and milk. At top, a herder slits the throat of an ox while a helper secures its bound feet; above, a farmer milks a tearful cow whose suckling calf has been tethered to its mother's leg to keep it from the udder.

Another source of nourishment for the people of the Nile lay teeming beneath the surface of its marshes. At bottom, a fisherman lowers his net to snare an oncoming mullet. To the right of the net, a fish has been caught on one of several hooks dangling from a single line, while to the left two crocodiles — heedless of the intruders — are locked throat to throat in a mating embrace.

their culture were mansions for the dead — huge structures that would stand as totems of the kingdoms' might long after the Egyptian cities were buried by the shifting sands.

The most astounding of these mountains of stone rose at Giza, on the west bank of the Nile some twenty miles north of the palace at Memphis. Commissioned around the year 2575 to house the remains of Khufu, the Fourth Dynasty pharaoh who would be known to later ages by the Greek name of Cheops, the epic construction absorbed the resources of the realm for much of the king's twenty-three-year reign. Ultimately, it would be celebrated not as Khufu's wonder but as the world's — a marvel acknowledged simply as the Great Pyramid.

It was laid out with geometric precision — a near-perfect square at the base, with sides of 755 feet that differed from each other by less than eight inches, and faces that sloped upward at an angle of fifty-one degrees to reach an apex nearly 500 feet above the desert floor. Into its construction went some 2,300,000 stone blocks averaging two and a half tons apiece, with many weighing as much as fifteen tons. The great limestone blocks of the facing had been cut with such skill that once they were in place, the blade of a knife could not be inserted between them. The result was an edifice that dwarfed the masterworks of later, more technologically sophisticated civilizations. (By one estimate, its area could contain the cathedrals of Florence and Milan alongside St. Peter's of Rome and St. Paul's of London, with room to spare.)

Near this monument on the Giza plateau, Khufu's son, Khafre, built his own massive pyramid. And beside it emerged the brooding figure of the Great Sphinx, an enigmatic stone effigy, 240 feet long from its haunches to its forepaws, with a lion's body and the visage of Khafre himself. A mythical beast that was revered as the guardian of sacred places, the Sphinx was shaped from an outcrop of rock left by Khufu's stonecutters.

In human as well as in material resources, the costs of the pyramid complexes of Khufu and Khafre were exorbitant. For more than twenty years, Khufu's quarrymen, using copper chisels and dolerite hammers, ceaselessly chipped away at the native stone to fashion the gigantic blocks that went into the pharaoh's monument. And over that same span, during the three months of the Nile's Inundation, when they would otherwise have been idle, a conscript army of 4,000 peasant laborers, lacking even the most elementary block and tackle, manhandled the great chunks from the main quarry sites at Tura and Aswan to the Nile, then floated them on barges to Giza. There, it is likely that wide earthen ramps had been built to run up the sides of the pyramid. When

Meat and fish were prized as delicacies in Egypt, but grain was the mainstay of the populace. Each year's harvest yielded vast quantities of bread and beer through labors of the sort depicted by these limestone figurines. Above, a servant woman strains barley mash through a sieve to produce fresh brew; at right, another woman grinds grain between two stones, making a flour that will be used for bread. On large estates, dozens of brewers and bakers would labor through the day to meet the needs of the household.

In a relief from the tomb of the Fifth Dynasty vizier Ptahhotep, servants carry a festive array of offerings for their master's eternal enjoyment — incl

...red livestock and flapping geese, bundles of papyrus stalks, and platters of fruit, loaves, and meat. Such scenes often showed the deceased enjoying the gifts at his table *(inset)*.

water was poured on the middle of the ramps, the resulting mud made an effective lubricant; then the workers, gaining traction on the dry shoulders, hauled the blocks into place with the help of palm-fiber ropes.

Such mammoth projects tested the limits of royal authority. In political and economic terms, the price of conscripting the gangs of laborers and supporting them through the years may well have been too high, because Khafre's successor, Menkaure, scaled down the dimensions of his own tomb. The last of the three pyramids built at Giza, it was scarcely one-third the size of its neighbors. But Menkaure would live on in Egyptian legend as a kind and pious figure, while Khufu and Khafre would be remembered as tyrants. The trend toward moderation continued with King Shepseskaf, who chose to erect a mastaba for his remains instead of a pyramid. This may have been part of a campaign by Shepseskaf to undermine the cult of the sun god Re, which was closely identified with the pyramid. If that was his object, he clearly failed; after his brief reign, a new royal line staunchly faithful to Re established itself at Heliopolis around the year 2475. The kings of the Fifth Dynasty returned to the pyramid form, although their tombs were relatively modest. More striking were the temples they erected to Re, shrines that included a central courtyard with an altar open to the sun and an enclosed chamber known as the Room of the Seasons, on whose walls artists portrayed the agricultural cycle made possible by the god's generous rays. Dominating the courtyard was an obelisk, rather squat at the base but tapering to a sharp point that mimicked the sunburst of the pyramids.

While attending to such sacred projects, the pharaohs did not neglect their worldly concerns. Like their predecessors, the kings of the Fifth and Sixth dynasties sponsored ambitious trading expeditions abroad. In contrast to Mesopotamia, where commerce had come early to a merchant class, the word for *merchant* did not even exist in Egypt until well into the second millennium. Instead, foreign trade was the province of the pharaoh, who commissioned royal ventures and hoped to reap royal profits.

One of the chief commodities sought by the king's agents was timber, for much of the wood needed to make furniture or provide beams for the villas of the wealthy had to be imported. A brisk trade had been conducted since the kingdom's early days with the ancient trading center of Byblos, on the coast of Lebanon near mountains studded with cedars. At first, the logs must have reached Egypt on foreign vessels, if only because the Egyptians had yet to accumulate a sufficient stock of timber to build their own seagoing fleet. While the Egyptians were among the world's earliest and best sailors, having acquired their skills on the great river, there is no record of their taking to the seas before the Fourth Dynasty, when King Sneferu ordered the construction of at least sixty merchant ships. Soon fleets of graceful galleys were sailing to Byblos. One of Sneferu's scribes recorded the "bringing of forty ships filled with cedar logs."

For other resources, the pharaohs looked south to Nubia, an area rich in gold, ivory, ebony, and animal pelts. Some of the most profitable expeditions were launched from the Aswan area by caravan leaders, who ventured deep into Africa at the king's behest. One such foray was undertaken by an Aswan noble named Harkhuf during the reign of King Pepy II, the last pharaoh of the Sixth Dynasty. At the journey's successful conclusion, Harkhuf wrote the king to inform him that he had returned with "great and beautiful gifts" for the pharaoh, including a "dancing dwarf . . . from the land of the spirits." Delighted by the news, Pepy II had an aide relay his instructions:

"Come northward to the court immediately; thou shalt bring this dwarf with thee,

Perched atop the throne of King Khafre, the falcon-god Horus embraces the pharaoh — his royal incarnation — in this masterpiece hewn of gem-hard diorite and polished smooth by the artist to capture the contours of the flesh. To protect the sacred statue after King Khafre's death, his attendants buried it in a deep pit beneath the floor of his temple at Giza.

The Great Sphinx guards the eastern approach to the Giza necropolis. The crouching beast bears the face of King Khafre, whose monument rises at center, between the Great Pyramid of his fa

fu, at right, and the smaller tomb of his successor, Menkaure. At the foot of Khufu's monument stand subsidiary pyramids, thought to house the remains of Khufu's queens.

which thou bringest living, prosperous and healthy from the land of the spirits, for the dances of the god, to rejoice and gladden the heart of the king of Upper and Lower Egypt, who lives forever. When he goes down with thee into the vessel, appoint excellent people, who shall be beside him on each side of the vessel; take care lest he fall into the water. When he sleeps at night appoint excellent people, who shall sleep beside him in his tent; inspect ten times a night. My majesty desires to see this dwarf more than the gifts of Sinai and of Punt."

The man behind this curious note was destined to preside over the end of an era in Egypt. Pepy II came to power as a boy around 2250 and, according to court records, ruled for more than ninety years. Though such a remarkable tenure should have given him more than enough material to swell his annals, he was not above taking credit for the feats of his predecessors. Inscribed on one wall of his temple were the names of Libyan chieftains captured by the pharaoh's forces — a list lifted verbatim from the tomb of the Fifth Dynasty's King Sahure, who had ruled some 200 years earlier.

Ultimately, Pepy II's long and increasingly decrepit reign may have exhausted the resources of his court: His own pyramid complex was massive enough to suit any king, but the surrounding tombs of his courtiers were shabby structures built of mud brick, suggesting that the royal retinue had fallen on hard times. In contrast, Egypt's nomarchs had been growing wealthy and powerful. Where formerly the provincial governors had been appointed by the pharaoh, the position was by now largely hereditary, and once entrenched, the scions of such local dynasties were less inclined to bow and scrape to the king. Indeed, a certain arrogance, unthinkable in previous centuries, crept into their relations with the pharaoh, as revealed by the statement of a nomarch at Hierankopolis: "I claimed from King Pepy II the honor of obtaining a sarcophagus, funerary wrappings, and oils for my father."

When Pepy II died, an epoch in the life of Egypt — later to be called the Old Kingdom — died with him. The country descended into turmoil. One severe blow to the people may well have been dealt by the natural force that had so long sustained them. Apparently, a slackening of the monsoon rains in the Ethiopian highlands led to a succession of low floods in Egypt. Crops failed, and mobs of starving vagrants pillaged the countryside; there was at least one account of cannibalism.

To Pepy's successors, whose authority, like that of all pharaohs, was based on their divine ability to draw forth the blessings of river, sun, and soil, the agricultural collapse was catastrophic. Within a span of twenty years, no fewer than twenty kings occupied the throne as Egypt lapsed into a period of feudal strife

The Bastion at Buhen

The architectural genius of the Egyptians was by no means confined to temples and tombs. During the occupation of northern Nubia by the kings of the Twelfth Dynasty, Egyptian engineers supervised the construction of one of the most forbidding fortresses of all time. Built around 1950 BC at Buhen, near the Nile's Second Cataract, it incorporated complex defenses that would not be surpassed for more than 3,000 years.

Ironically, this masterwork — one of a string of forts along the frontier — was an outgrowth of the era of anarchy from which Egypt had recently emerged. During that bloody epoch, local chieftains had begun to protect their strongholds with deep ditches and high walls. The builders of the Buhen fortress applied those same principles, constructing two massive barriers of mud brick — an outer bulwark and an inner wall ringing the garrison (diagram, following page). Both parapets were protected by ditches and notched with thousands of loopholes — downward-sloping crevices through which archers could fire on attackers with relative impunity.

Secure within the ramparts, the governor of the occupied territory tended to its affairs, seeing that gold from Nubian mines and copper smelted near the fortress reached the pharaoh's storerooms in Egypt. At his two-story residence not far from the barracks, the governor received sensitive dispatches on papyrus scrolls that were later shredded by clerks. And periodically he climbed a stairway from his house to the top of the battlements to oversee the defenses. For more than 200 years the fortress remained impregnable. It fell into hostile hands only after Egypt was invaded by Asiatic warriors and relaxed its grip on Nubia.

The projecting battlements of the outer wall at Buhen defied assault: Troops who survived the storm of arrows from the loopholes would be met at the wall by stones rained from above.

that would last 100 years. Long after it ended, that awful period would resound in legend, serving as the basis for countless cautionary tales. One such narrative, written centuries later under the title "Admonitions of a Sage," presented a lurid picture of social disintegration:

"The rabble is elated, and from every city goes up the cry: 'Come! let us throw out the aristocrats!' The land is full of rioters. When the ploughman goes to work he takes a shield with him.

"Everything is filthy: there is no such thing as clean linen these days. The dead are thrown into the river. People abandon the city and live in tents. Buildings are fired, though the Palace still stands. But Pharaoh is kidnapped by the mob.

"The ladies of the nobility exclaim, 'If only we had something to eat!' They are embarrassed when someone greets them. They are forced to prostitute their daughters. They are reduced to sleeping with men who were once too badly off to take a woman."

As might be expected under such conditions, government was a matter of brute force. Nomarchs, ruling as feudal barons in their own domains, clashed frequently with their neighbors or formed fragile alliances to fight other loose confederations. The air of conflict extended even to the once-tranquil realm of the dead: One nomarch was buried with wooden figurines of lancers and archers, who in the afterworld would presumably render him the same service that they had on earth.

For much of this fractious time in Egypt, a powerful line of nomarchs held sway in Herakleopolis, fifty-five miles south of Memphis. Their pretensions to the title of pharaoh began with one Akhthoes, who according to a later text, sought power "by great cruelty which wrought woes for Egypt." His successors, the kings of the Ninth and Tenth dynasties, ruled under constant challenge, especially from an able and belligerent family in Thebes, far up the Nile and well removed from the seat of Old Kingdom authority. Finally around 2065, after a century of brawling, the Thebans under Mentuhotpe II fought their way downriver and defeated the Herakleopolitans.

Though they succeeded in reuniting Egypt, the Thebans held power for only three generations, with the last ruler giving way under mysterious circumstances to his own vizier, Ammenemes, who may have staged a coup. Once in power, Ammenemes distanced himself from the Thebans by establishing a new capital near Memphis, where he hoped to emulate the majesty of earlier pharaohs. But he was frustrated in

Situated on the west bank of the Nile, the Buhen fortress was frequented by Egyptian warships and trading vessels. The fortress comprised several districts: the soldiers' barracks, a commercial area, the official quarter, and a temple dedicated to Horus of Buhen, patron of the outpost. Before a siege, a drawbridge located within the west gate of the garrison wall (below, center) would be retracted on rollers; the garrison could still communicate with the outside world by means of a tunnel.

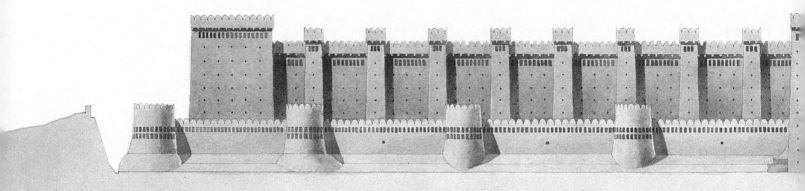

that ambition by the defiant nomarchs, some of whom still had their own armies and fleets. Ultimately, the beleaguered king was murdered by conspirators within his court. At the time of the assassination, Ammenemes' son, Sesostris, who had been named coregent several years before, was on a military campaign. Rushing back to court, he managed to assert his rightful claim to the throne.

Among the many talents of Sesostris I and his Twelfth Dynasty successors was the ability to learn from the past. Cautiously, patiently, they whittled away at the vexing power of the nomarchs; it took about 150 years to complete the task, but the provincial governors were at last reduced to nominal authority.

In their religious building projects, the Twelfth Dynasty kings could be lavish, as evidenced by the splendid temples they erected to Amun, now risen from his humble position as the local Theban deity to rank as lord of lords. Yet in their mortuary complexes, the same pharaohs were careful to avoid the excesses of the Old Kingdom. Their pyramids were poorly made, with interiors of mud brick and casing stones that were sometimes stolen from the pyramids of their predecessors.

Above all, the Twelfth Dynasty rulers were aware of the consequences that could follow successive failures of the Nile, and they were tireless in their efforts to conserve the life-giving waters: Sesostris II began an ambitious irrigation project in the fertile Faiyum region, southwest of Memphis. Completed under Ammenemes III, it consisted of a canal 300 feet wide leading from the Nile to a 670-square-mile natural depression. The flow of water into that basin was controlled by a dam with sluice gates. When the Nile flooded, the gates would be opened and the basin would fill. The reservoir's waters would help irrigate the Faiyum through the dry months ahead.

The pharaohs of this era were equally energetic in pursuing foreign trade. Among the most ambitious of the commercial expeditions they sponsored were those to a realm that Egyptian scribes called Punt, located on the East African coast near present-day Somalia. To reach Punt — source of frankincense, myrrh, and other fragrant resins used by the Egyptians during their religious ceremonies — caravans had first to complete an eight-day trek across the blazing eastern desert from Koptos on the Upper Nile to the Red Sea. To complicate matters, the conscripts assigned to the task had to carry with them the dismantled sections of the ship that would bear them southward down the African coast. The leader of one such expedition described the ordeal in the matter-of-fact tone generally adopted by Egyptian officials in their reports: ''My lord sent me to dispatch a ship to Punt to bring him back fresh myrrh. I left with an army of 3,000 men. Every day I issued to each a leathern bottle, two jars of water, 20 pieces of bread. Then I reached the Red Sea, made the ship and dispatched it.''

Another tempting commercial target lay south along the Nile. Pushing troops into Nubia, the Twelfth Dynasty kings extended the Egyptian frontier as far as the Third Cataract, about 450 miles beyond Aswan, thereby bringing under their control a region rich in gold. To consolidate their gains, the invaders built at Buhen a great fortress, bristling with battlements. And by the Nile at nearby Semna, a towering statue of Sesostris III was erected to encourage submission in all those who gazed on it. Forsaking the time-honored convention of representing the pharaoh with an expres-

sionless mask, the sculptors endowed Sesostris with a careworn look — eyelids heavy and mouth tightly set, as if to convey to friend and foe alike the impression of a man who took his imperial mission seriously.

In the Mediterranean, meanwhile, Egyptian vessels acquired wealth for the kingdom through more peaceable means, increasing the long-standing traffic with Byblos and other centers of Palestine and establishing new trading ties with the opulent Minoan culture of Crete. Thus the Egyptians assured themselves a steady influx of such prized items as timber and olive oil in exchange for their surplus stores of flax, papyrus, salted fish, ox hide, alabaster, and gold.

And then, just as it appeared that this epoch was attaining full flower, it began to wither. Apparently the Twelfth Dynasty simply died out, for King Ammenemes IV was followed around 1785 by the obscure Queen Nefrusobek, whose brief term ended the proud line. As many as seventy pharaohs followed over the next 150 years — a period that saw a renewal of rivalry between Upper and Lower Egypt. Once again, the Nile may have undermined the pharaoh's prestige, this time with excessive floods.

The weakening of central authority left Egypt ill-prepared to deal with a foreign challenge. Yet just such a prospect was brewing in the Near East, and before long the troubled land of the Nile would be confronted with the prospect of invasion.

Over the centuries, the Egyptians had managed to hold at bay the warlike tribes along their borders — the formidable Nubians to the south, the bedouins of the eastern desert, and the Libyans to the west. Indeed, the Egyptians often turned the ferocity of their adversaries to good use by inducting those they captured into the pharaoh's army. Yet none of this advanced the technology of warfare in Egypt. Centuries after Mesopotamian warriors had begun to use helmets and armor, sturdy axes, and composite bows made of laminated strips whose strength and flexibility provided superior range, Egyptian soldiers still clung to javelins and simple bows and fought nearly nude, relying on cumbersome, man-size shields to fend off blows or missiles.

The incursion that finally exposed Egypt's vulnerability was part of a vast migration touched off around the year 1800 by warlike tribes moving from the steppes of Asia into the Middle East. The initial effect of this upheaval on Egypt was innocent enough: Exiles from Palestine and more distant parts began to swell the population of the Delta. Some of the new arrivals were slaves who had been sold into bondage or had surrendered their freedom in exchange for economic protection. Then, around 1650, the Delta was engulfed by Asiatic warriors referred to by the Egyptians as the Hyksos, or "rulers from foreign lands." Clad in body armor and wielding scimitars and bows, they rode to war in a revolutionary vehicle unknown to Egypt — a two-wheeled chariot that confounded the efforts of mere foot soldiers.

Badly outmatched, the pharaoh's forces put up little resistance. "I do not know why God was displeased with us," wrote an Egyptian priest of a later generation. "Unexpectedly from the regions of the East came men of unknown race. Confident of victory, they marched against our land. By force they took it, easily, without a single battle."

Secure in their Delta stronghold, the Hyksos declined to occupy Upper Egypt and merely exacted tribute from the ruling families there. Yet by filling their coffers in this way, the Hyksos kings were ensuring their own demise. For 100 years, resentment festered in the south, until Thebes once again resisted the demands of the north. From that defiant city on the Nile, finally, a prince would emerge at the head of a revitalized army to crush the Hyksos and forge a mighty new kingdom — one whose grandeur would be impressed on its neighbors by force.

LAST RITES OF ROYALTY

In death as in life, a wide gulf separated the rulers of the first civilizations from their subjects. To be sure, kings were not the only ones to aspire to an afterlife: The practice of equipping the dead with food and drink for the journey to the next world was embraced in many lands and at all levels of society. Yet royalty, in preparing for death, laid claim to far more than sustenance. The ultimate goal of their lavish rites was to maintain their exalted status forever, an ambition that often led to reckless expenditures of treasure, toil, and blood.

Kings desired to reign eternal even when prevailing beliefs about the afterlife gave them no encouragement. The netherworld as conceived by the Sumerians was, by most accounts, a dreary place where harsh gods held sway over the meek and the mighty alike. In the Sumerian *Epic of Gilgamesh,* a dying warrior recounts his nightmare vision of the palace of Ereshkigal, goddess of the underworld: "I entered the house of dust and I saw the kings of the earth, their crowns put away forever. They who had stood in the place of gods stood now like servants to fetch baked meats in the house of dust." Such gloomy forebodings appear not to have troubled members of the royal family at Ur, who went to the grave with dozens of their own retainers, sacrificed for the occasion. The rulers of Ur may have seen themselves as divine beings who were entitled to take the lives of their devotees. And perhaps they envisioned an afterlife in which they would command the eternal loyalty of their subjects.

No such perplexities surround the last rites conducted for the kings of Egypt in the days of the pyramids. In stark contrast to the services performed in the death pits at Ur, the ceremony enacted at the Great Pyramid was designed to free the pharaoh from the earth and its forces of decay and launch him heavenward. He alone was entitled to follow in the radiant path of the sun god, so there was no cause for those in his retinue to be sacrificed: The king would carry on in splendid isolation.

Whatever realm they were destined for in the next life, rulers were sent on their way with fabulous treasures. Inevitably, such troves lured thieves, whose deeds compounded the mystery surrounding royal gravesites. The fact that neither a body nor grave goods were found in the king's chamber of the Great Pyramid, for example, has led to speculation that the pharaoh was buried elsewhere. The weight of the evidence, however, indicates that his corpse and treasures were indeed deposited in the chamber but were later plundered. Like other rulers who aspired to high places in the next life, the pharaoh was apparently brought down in time by predators.

Around the year 2550 BC in the Sumerian city-state of Ur, a royal cemetery located near the city's ziggurat became the setting for a series of grim rites in which scores of retainers were sacrificed to join their master in the next world. Within a century or two, at least sixteen such ceremonies were performed to mark the death of members of the royal family. The funeral portrayed here and on the following two pages was carried out for a man whose name has been lost to history but who apparently was a king; in the ceremony, sixty-three people were put to death. Judging by the orderly disposition of their remains, the victims played their part obediently to the end, looking forward, perhaps, to some reward in the afterlife.

Preparations for the king's burial began with the digging of a great pit more than thirty feet deep and nearly as long. An earthen ramp was built down into the pit, and at one end of the space, masons set to work on the king's tomb chamber. Once the chamber was finished, attendants stocked it with precious offerings, including model boats fashioned of copper and silver. Then the body of the king was placed in the tomb along with a few of his personal servants — the first people in his retinue to be sacrificed — and the entrance was sealed.

There followed a cortege of victims down the ramp: elegant women of the court, their hair bound in a net of gold ribbon and crowned with silver rosettes; guards with daggers sheathed at their belts; and musicians bearing two great lyres whose sound boxes were ornamented with bull's heads. Near the end of the procession, grooms coaxed two teams of oxen yoked to four-wheeled chariots backward down the ramp, followed by six helmeted soldiers with copper spears. Each of the victims bore a cup. In sacramental fashion, they probably received a poison to drink. Through it all, the musicians strummed their lyres — until their own limbs were stilled by the drug.

DESCENT TO THE GRAVE

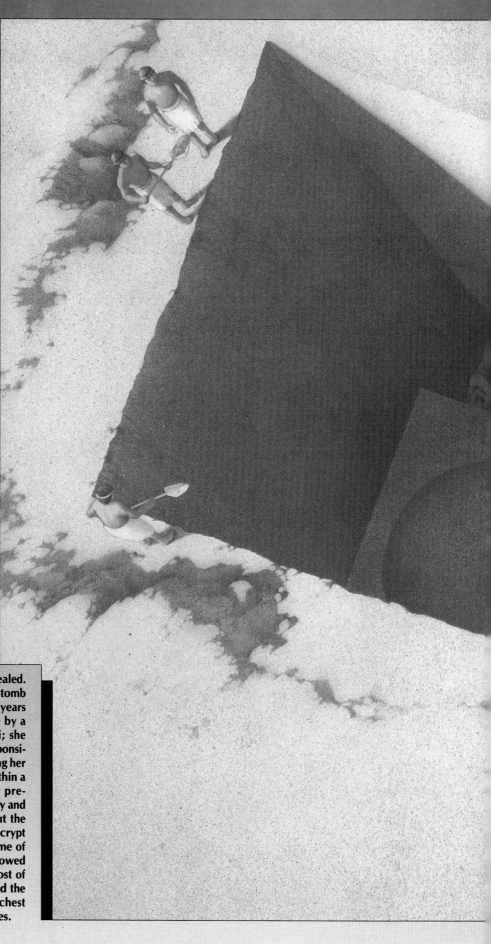

Once the initial sacrifice at Ur had been completed, attendants wielding shovels started the slow process of filling in the death pit of the king. The work proceeded in stages. In the first ceremony, the victims, who were lying in close formation around the vaulted tomb chamber, were covered by several feet of earth. Then the attendants deposited a layer of clay and tamped it down to provide a floor for a second ceremony: To hallow the ground that had just been laid, priests slaughtered sacrificial animals, poured libations, and offered up yet another human life. The ritual was repeated, level by level, until the pit was sealed. Despite all these exertions, the king's tomb did not long remain inviolate. A few years later, he was followed to the grave by a woman identified on a seal as Puabi; she was evidently his queen, for those responsible for her burial were intent on placing her close to the king. Digging down to within a few feet of his tomb chamber, they prepared a new pit to receive Puabi's body and those of dozens of her attendants. But the proximity of the king's richly stocked crypt proved too great a temptation for some of the gravediggers, who furtively burrowed into the nearby tomb and pilfered most of its treasures. Then they coolly covered the shaft with Puabi's heavy wardrobe chest and carried on with their solemn duties.

Even as Sumerian workers hollowed out the death pits at Ur, gangs of Egyptian conscripts were raising up the Great Pyramid of Khufu at Giza. With the passing of the pharaoh around the year 2550, the ceremony whose arrangements had absorbed the king and thousands of his subjects for two decades was at last set in motion.

First the body of the pharaoh was ferried up the Nile from the palace at Memphis to Giza, a distance of twenty miles. The bark that carried Khufu's remains was probably a high-prowed cedar vessel, built to resemble the mythical papyrus skiff paddled each day across the heavens by the sun god Re: Vessels of that sort were later buried in pits next to the pyramid to enable the pharaoh's spirit to accompany Re on his daily round.

On reaching Giza, the priests and mourners entered the valley temple, near the water's edge, to begin the lengthy rites. No one who witnessed the ceremony ever revealed its mysteries, but the services performed there probably revolved around several majestic statues of the pharaoh. By rubbing a statue's lips with milk and touching them with the sculptor's tools and other charmed implements, priests could prepare that particular effigy to serve as a protector of the pharaoh's spirit.

In the next stage of the procession, the king's remains were carried up an enclosed causeway — past mastabas and subsidiary pyramids prepared for the king's trusted advisers and consorts — to the courtyard of a mortuary temple at the base of the pyramid. There, offerings of food and drink were left at a shrine for the deceased, to be replenished daily for years to come. Then at last the pallbearers entered the sacred recesses of the pyramid to entrust their master to his eternal home.

BURYING THE GOD-KING

The funeral procession for the pharaoh Khufu culminated at the king's chamber, deep within the Great Pyramid. Bearing the mummified body of their lord in a wooden casket and his vital organs in a separate container known as a canopic chest, the priests and attendants first ascended a steep passageway of polished limestone known as the grand gallery. From the head of that lofty corridor the celebrants crept through a small opening, grappling with their precious cargo, to reach an antechamber and the cavernous vault beyond.

Built for the ages, the king's chamber was faced with the hardest of stones — dark granite, carved at Aswan 450 miles away and floated down the Nile by barge to Giza. Waiting in the vault to receive the casket was the pharaoh's sarcophagus, which had been placed there during the construction of the pyramid.

By the flickering light of an oil lamp, the pallbearers completed their task, depositing the casket with a final prayer and setting down the canopic chest nearby. The organs it contained were to be of service to the body in the afterlife. All that remained was to secure the tomb against invaders. As the last of the celebrants withdrew, workers sealed off the grand gallery: Massive stone blocks, stored on a platform aloft, were eased onto the floor of the gallery and released down the grooved runway to plug the entrance below. The workers then exited through a narrow escape chute, which they sealed behind them. No one knows what treasures were left in Khufu's chamber to fortify him in the afterlife: Despite the elaborate precautions taken, the tomb was eventually plundered, leaving a vacant space deep within the world's most ambitious monument.

A diagram of the Great Pyramid reveals three successive schemes for the pharaoh's burial chamber. Workers first prepared a descending passage to a subterranean vault. Then they changed plans, forged an ascending passageway, and began work on a second chamber in the monument. Before it could be completed, Khufu authorized an even more ambitious scheme. The ascending passageway was extended and expanded to become the grand gallery. It led to the imposing king's chamber, which was reinforced above by a gable of granite slabs.

AIR SHAFT

AIR SHAFT

KING'S CHAMBER

GRAND
GALLERY

ESCAPE CHUTE

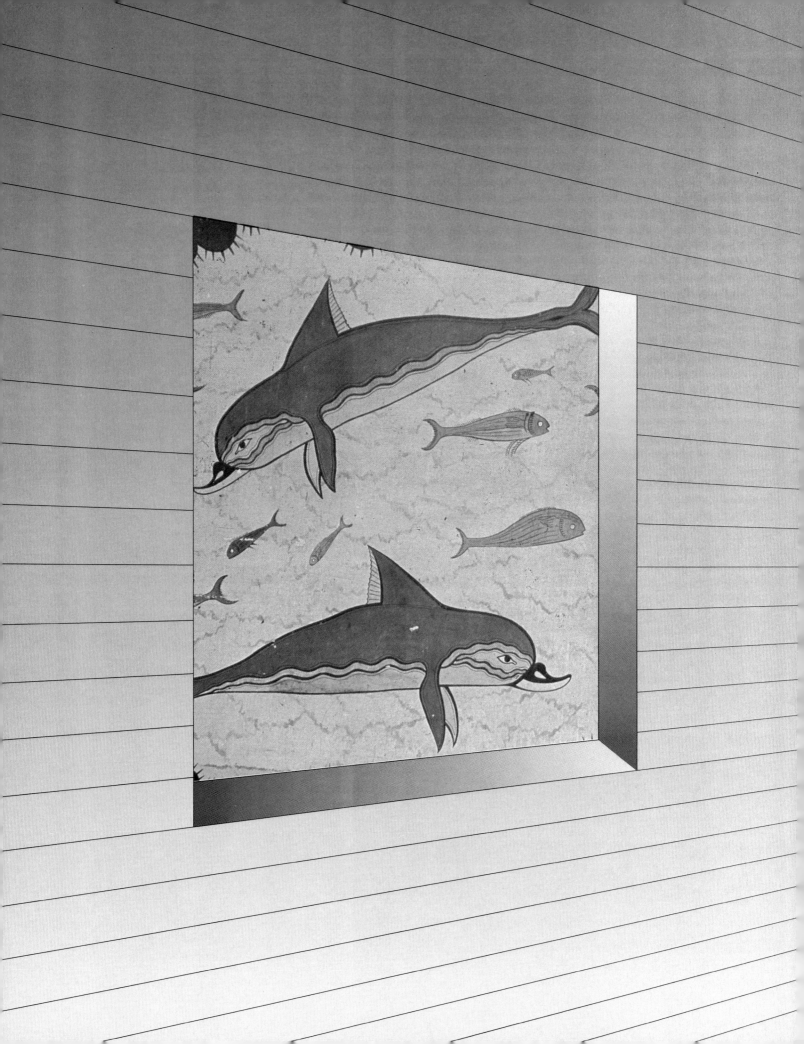

THE EMPIRE ON THE AEGEAN

3 Nobody knows how the first settlers reached Crete, the 152-mile-long, whale-shaped island in the eastern Mediterranean that would become, beginning about 1900 BC, the scene of the most vivacious of all early civilizations. It is not known, for that matter, who the first Cretans were or where they came from — only that they arrived in the seventh millennium BC.

One ancient tradition says they embarked from the tail end of Europe — the Greek mainland. A strong wind often blows from the north, from Greece toward Crete. Perhaps early mariners, hugging the jagged Greek shoreline, and anxiously trying to navigate from one protective cove to the next, suddenly found themselves being driven southward by a gale. Whirled past the Cyclades, the islands that dot the southern Aegean like steppingstones, the voyagers would have made landfall on Crete's northern shore.

On the other hand, the first Cretans may have been seaborne people from the Levant — the coastal areas of today's Israel, Lebanon, and Syria — or from Turkey, or even from Egypt or Libya in Africa. The strong counterclockwise current that sweeps through the eastern Mediterranean could well have grabbed any clumsy craft sailing out too far from any of these shores and carried it willy-nilly in a northwesterly direction toward the Aegean and Crete.

In all likelihood, Crete was originally settled by mariners from a number of these areas. Whatever their point of departure may have been, the Neolithic voyagers, huddling wet and miserable in their tiny vessels, would have taken comfort in their first sighting of Crete. With the peaks of three mountains rising out of the sea like the three-pronged trident of a powerful god, the island appeared not only substantial but inviting as well.

But the island proved a mixed blessing. It was a wild place of jumbled hills, ragged limestone peaks and tangled gorges — difficult terrain for cultivation. Rivers on Crete were mere streams compared with the Nile or the Euphrates, unsuitable as sources of irrigation; and there were no floodplains to ease the farmers' tasks.

For all its deficits, Crete did possess three great agricultural assets: abundant sunlight, adequate rain, and fertile, if rocky, soil. The settlers, intermarrying and living in permanent villages, shared the special skills and farming techniques they had brought from their various homelands and made the most of the island's gifts. Over the centuries, they planted fields of barley and wheat in the protected valleys. In time, they discovered that the sun-drenched hillsides were ideal for grapevines and that the climate also suited olive trees: Crete's future prosperity would be based on exports of wine and olive oil.

They also learned that what the Egyptians feared as the Great Green Sea was to be their best friend. The encircling expanses of water provided a natural barrier against invaders. Neither early in their settlement of the island nor later during the height of Cretan civilization did the people find it necessary to build protective walls around their towns and cities.

And while the Mediterranean discouraged would-be conquerors, the Cretans increasingly used it as a highway for commerce and as a means to extend their own influence. The island's sure-handed shipwrights and sailors launched the first merchant marine in the ancient world. Cretan seafarers developed colonies throughout the Aegean; the island's traders carried their search for profits many hundreds of miles — to Egypt, the Cyclades, and Syria. From Sumerian technology, the Cretans learned the secret of bronze making, and from the Egyptians, the art of stone vase making. In the prosperity brought by a bustling trade, architects and engineers designed harbor facilities, aqueducts, and splendid palaces.

Perhaps because of their isolation, the people of Crete gave far less thought to weapons and war than did their contemporaries in Egypt and Mesopotamia. Unlike the Egyptians, who covered the walls of their tombs with scenes of official pomp and pageantry, or the Sumerians, who left a visual record of their conquests, Crete's artists painted idyllic scenes of people at leisure or engaged in sports. They also decorated walls with pictures of flowers, fish, birds, and dolphins. The Cretans were a people who seemed joyously immersed in the present, in the wonders of life on their small island. And when at last, after 1,000 years of civilization, they succumbed to earthquake and invasion, they left no decipherable record of their history and few other traces of their times.

What the Cretans achieved had no parallel anywhere else in Europe. From the craggy coasts of Ireland to the rocky shores of Greece, most people still lived as they had since the dawn of humanity, roaming in clans, hunting animals and birds, and gathering wild plants to eat. From place to place, family groups had forsaken the nomadic life to begin farming in a rudimentary way, but nowhere in Europe had humans undertaken the sort of agriculture that could lead to surplus crops and the creation of a civilization.

The accomplishments on Crete were so isolated, in fact, that they almost went unnoticed by history. The people of Crete were remembered only in myths until, thirty-three centuries after their civilization died, the secrets that lay buried beneath their fallen palaces were finally unlocked.

Much of what has been learned about this extraordinary culture is owed to Sir Arthur Evans who, beginning in March of 1900, uncovered the forgotten civilization. A British scholar who was enchanted by Greek history, Evans began his archeological adventure more or less by accident. In Athens, a dealer in antiquities showed Evans a number of tiny, engraved personal seals said to have been found on Crete. Evans had a sharp eye for detail, and a close look at these ancient curiosities revealed what he described as "squiggles." Believing that the strange marks were some kind of writing and that he was on the trail of a long-dead and -forgotten language, Evans started out for Crete to hunt for more of the seals. Eventually, his search carried him to the small and seemingly insignificant Cretan village of Knossos where, on a hunch, he undertook the excavation of a large mound of debris. The mound turned out to be ruins of an enormous palace.

In time, the spades and shovels of Evans's workers unearthed fragments of a fresco — a procession of men holding an assortment of lovely pots and vases. The serene figures, brought to light after thousands of years of burial, fascinated Evans. Here was his first look at the people who had built this fine palace. Here, also, was the link that would help him identify his find and place it properly in the chain of human history. Evans knew the Egyptians had painted similar figures on the walls of tombs in the royal city of Thebes. Dating from around 1500 BC, the Egyptian tomb frescoes depicted processions of foreigners bringing gifts for the Pharaoh Tuthmosis III. In sharp contrast to their short-tressed Egyptian hosts, these exotic strangers wore their hair in long locks falling over their shoulders. Bare-chested and slender, they were dressed in high-laced boots and loincloths or in intricately patterned kilts that hung lower in front. Among the offerings they carried were elaborately decorated vases with graceful, curved handles; delicate bowls and ewers of gold and silver; long, necklacelike chains; and — very unusual in Egypt — offering vessels in the shape of a bull's head. Hieroglyphics beside the paintings recorded that the visitors had been welcomed as "chiefs of the Keftiu and the isles in the midst of the sea."

The men in the frescoes at Knossos looked much like the giftbearers at Thebes — the same kilts, the same flowing locks of dark hair. Evans was sure he had found the home of the Keftiu, a people known and respected by the Egyptians. The dates assigned by

Europe's first civilization evolved on Crete, a long, narrow island situated at the southern entrance of the Aegean Sea. Crete was home to the Minoans, a seafaring people who, beginning about 2000 BC, built an empire based on maritime trade. Taking full advantage of their strategic location in the Mediterranean, Minoan mariners forged trade routes to Egypt, Libya, Palestine, Asia Minor, mainland Greece, and the islands of the Aegean. Many of their trading posts developed into full-fledged colonies, extending Minoan influence throughout the Aegean and eastern Mediterranean.

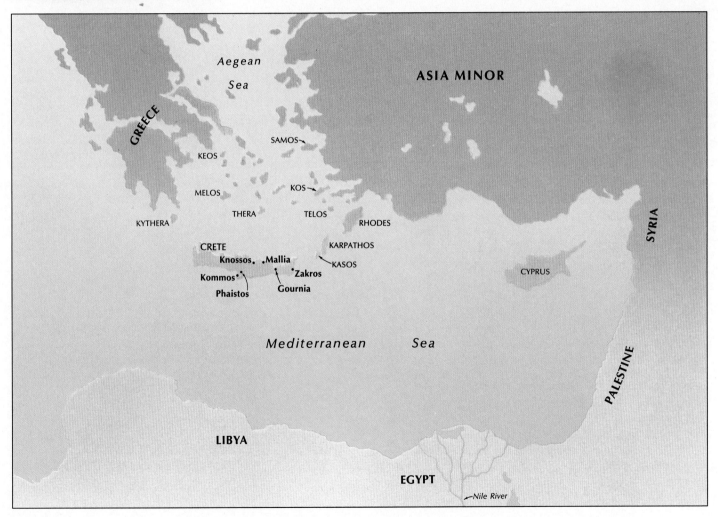

archeologists to pottery shards collected at the Knossos site indicated that the palace was incredibly old. Its construction about 1900 BC predated the early Mycenaean Greeks, who, according to legend, had fought and won the Trojan War. Evans was convinced that he had stumbled onto the remains of a highly developed society, perhaps the earliest civilization in Europe.

Devoting more than thirty years of his life to the restoration of the palace at Knossos, Evans continually delighted the world with reports of handsome palace frescoes, sweeping staircases, tapered columns, and intricate freshwater conduits. But his efforts to learn more about the civilization that had created these splendors turned out to be frustrating at times. His excavation yielded a hoard of clay tablets containing a mysterious script — the squiggles he had seen on the personal seals at Athens. Yet, even after decades of study, Evans was unable to make sense of the writing. In fact, the script, which he referred to as Linear A, is so unlike any other system of writing, it has never been deciphered. Consequently, little or nothing is known about the poetry and politics of the people who once wrote in Linear A. Pieced together from bits of smashed artwork and from other evidence found in the tumbled ruins, Cretan history remains no more than fragmentary. Much of the story, as it is now interpreted, is based on surmise. Even the name given to the Cretan culture was drawn from the language and legends of later people, the Greeks.

Evans called his Bronze Age island-dwellers the Minoans, after King Minos, an Aegean ruler prominent in Greek myth. According to legend, Zeus, the king of the gods, fell in love with a beautiful mortal named Europa, a princess from Palestine. He appeared to her first in the shape of a bull and later as an eagle, and she bore him several sons — among them Minos. Establishing a fabulous kingdom on Crete, Minos commanded a large navy, swept the sea of pirates, and imposed his will on the peoples who lived along the coast of the Aegean. He exacted heavy tribute from the conquered cities. Every year, Athens was forced to send him a ship filled with young men and women; they were fed to a creature called the Minotaur. Part bull and part man, this monster lurked in the labyrinth, a building so diabolically intricate in construction that no one who entered could find a way out again. In one famous story, the Athenian hero Theseus unwound a ball of thread as he stalked the Minotaur through the twisting passages of the labyrinth. After slaying the bull-man with a magic sword given him by Minos's love-stricken daughter, Ariadne, Theseus returned along the trail of the thread and escaped.

The Minoans sailed easily before the Mediterranean winds. Their first watercraft were probably crude dugout canoes suited only for coastwise voyaging. But by the beginning of the second millennium, they had learned to build and to sail much more seaworthy vessels. From highland forests of oak, cypress, cedar, and fir, skilled shipwrights cut lumber for masts, keels, and planking. The vessels were then assembled at water's edge along the coves that indented Crete's coastline.

The Minoans preserved images of their vessels in carvings on the stone or clay personal seals that sailors carried for identification. Some of the seals depict galleys with high prows, low sterns, rounded hulls, and a single square sail. Some were also shown with a large oarlike rudder in the stern and sometimes with a small deck cabin. When the wind died, oarsmen, numbering up to twenty-five on each side, were the sole means of propulsion for these ships.

The Minoan vessels were far superior to any other craft on the Mediterranean, including the shore-hugging boats favored by the Egyptians. The high prows of the Minoan ships turned aside wave crests and kept the vessels from swamping; the heavy construction prevented the ships from breaking up under the punishment of pounding seas; and their massive, deep keels provided stability. In such vessels Minoan sailors could ride out all but the fiercest of Mediterranean squalls and sail safely for weeks on the open sea.

With the help of their sturdy vessels, Minoans became the preeminent sea traders of their times. The seafaring islanders used their ships and their central location in the eastern Mediterranean to link several major centers of trade. The Cyclades and the coast of Asia Minor lay only a few days' sail to the northeast. Mainland Greece, to the northwest, was only 190 miles away. Less than 400 miles to the southeast, the rich Nile Delta beckoned, and 600 miles to the east, Cyprus, Syria, and Palestine all lay within reach of Crete's stout merchant vessels.

From harbors on the northern, eastern, and southern coasts of Crete, ships embarked

On the south coast of Crete, near the base of a chalk white headland, lay the port of Kommos, one of the busiest of all the Minoan harbor installations. Here as at other Minoan ports, single-masted trading vessels loaded and unloaded cargoes directly onto the shore. Stevedores plied the sandy beach, shifting the goods to and from warehouses in which mountains of commodities were stored. The structure at upper left, adjacent to the warehouses, may have been an enclosure for protecting vessels during the winter months. From Kommos, imported commodities were hauled to the nearby towns of Hagia Triadha and Phaistos, where the inhabitants were the chief beneficiaries of the port's trade.

with cargoes of timber, olive oil, wine, glazed pottery, stone jars, clay lamps, and woolen cloth as well as bronze daggers and hammered silver from artisans' workshops. In exchange for these goods, the islanders acquired copper from Cyprus; gold, ivory, precious stones, plumes, and textiles from Egypt; silver from Greece; and obsidian from the Aegean isles. In Syria, they bartered for tin and lapis lazuli, which had come by caravan from central Asia. The Minoans sweetened their profits by serving as intermediaries or brokers between other peoples. For instance, it is likely that the Egyptian pharaohs imported cedar from Syria in ships sailed by the Minoans.

Through trade, the Minoans extended their influence in disparate regions of the eastern Mediterranean. At ports along their established network of commercial routes they succeeded in planting rootstocks of their culture. Some of these sites were intended to be no more than outposts for traders. Others were full-fledged colonies, with governors and civil officials sent from Crete to run the affairs of the populace. Some of these colonies were born of political exigencies: If a ruler of an island touched by

Minoan influence found himself pressured by rivals or outright enemies, he would call for assistance from the Minoan fleet. If the Minoans responded, their help would come at a price — allegiance to Crete.

The Minoans set up colonies throughout the Cyclades — including the islands of Thera, Melos, and Keos — and put down roots on the mainland of Greece. They also reached more distant latitudes, hopscotching to Kasos, Karpathos, Rhodes, Telos, Kos, and Samos and thence to the mainland of Asia Minor. They may have ranged as far as Sicily, where legend says Minos was killed while on a military expedition. To avenge a sacrilege, Minos and his fleet had rushed to Sicily in pursuit of Daedalus, the Greek genius who had designed the labyrinth. Determined to avoid capture, Daedalus secretly rigged a pipe and helped the enemies of Minos pour a caldron of boiling water onto the king while he luxuriated in a warm bath. Minos's followers honored their slain leader by founding a city on Sicily and naming it Minoa.

The Minoans controlled the seas surrounding their homeland with solid confidence. Although they apparently had no full-time navy, their large merchant fleet was probably armed to defend itself against pirates and strong enough to protect Crete from invasion or surprise attack by sea raiders. In any case, no people who lived within striking distance of Crete had had the inclination or the ability to take on the Minoans as adversaries. The peoples of mainland Greece were landsmen and therefore presented no military threat to Crete. Nor was Egypt in a position to challenge the kings of Crete on the sea. Most of the pharaoh's vessels were suited only for the Nile, and his relatively small fleet of seagoing ships rarely ventured beyond Syria.

In fact, the Egyptians, who typically showed no great love of strangers, respected the Minoans for their prowess as seafarers and traders. Foreigners in general were known to the pharaohs as *Ha-unebu,* which means "people from beyond the seas"; and foreigners were at times described as "barbarians who are an abomination to God." Only the people of Crete and its colonies were honored and distinguished with a separate name — the Keftiu.

During the early centuries of Crete's rise to political and commercial power, the island was split into a number of independent principalities, each with its own great palace. But by 1450 BC, the regional princes who lived in these elegantly decorated edifices had fallen under the sway of the king at Knossos. This king's name was Minos also, an appellation that may have been common to all the rulers of Crete. King Minos ruled from an immense palace that faced the Aegean from the crest of a low hill about three miles inland. Rebuilt following a calamitous earthquake in about 1600 BC, the Knossos palace was a multilevel complex of corridors, columns, and sweeping staircases — all encompassing a large central courtyard. Some of the ideas expressed in its architecture may have been borrowed from a palace at Mari, a Mesopotamian city visited by traders from Crete. But unlike builders in Sumer and Egypt, the Minoans disdained symmetry; architects at Knossos filled their palace with rooms of different sizes and shapes, connecting them with hallways that jutted off in all directions. Many of the interior walls consisted of multiple doors that could be opened to change the shape of a room. To Greeks and other foreigners who were unfamiliar with its layout, the palace must have seemed an enigmatic jumble — indeed, a labyrinth.

Perhaps most suggestive of the Minotaur's maze was the palace's multistory west wing, where the king and his family lived in great luxury. Leading to the upper floors was a winding staircase resting on a forest of tapered wooden columns. These and other palace columns were larger at the top than at the bottom, a convention that perhaps evolved because the tree trunks originally used to support roofs in Crete were inverted to keep them from taking root in the earthen floors. Above the stairs was one of the palace's many light-wells, openings in the roof that channeled sunlight into the building. At each landing, the stairway opened onto a colonnaded veranda overlooking a lush garden.

Religious ceremonies were performed in a lovely but unimposing hall that featured a single, high-backed alabaster chair — the oldest throne in Europe. Here a priestess sat flanked by the ranking authorities, who arranged themselves on stone benches. A pair of griffins, part of a fresco on the wall behind the throne, embellished the scene. On the floor opposite the throne, a lustral basin — a sunken chamber surrounded by a balustrade — and a collection of sacred stone vessels waited to be put to use in purification rites as well as in other traditional ceremonies.

For Minoans, religion and government were closely related. The bull symbol, associated both with Crete's religion and with its ruler, pervaded palace artwork. As they entered the palace, visitors were confronted with a giant fresco of a charging bull that dominated the east wall. Stylized horns, carved from massive blocks of stone, consecrated the rooms and hallways where they stood. Palace officials poured libations from vessels fashioned into the shape of a bull's head. On ceremonial occasions, the king may have worn a bull mask and, in this manner, created the legend of the Minotaur.

The king's religious duties may have made him godlike in the eyes of his people. But he had another role to play, and this was likely the true source of his power. He was the island's chief businessman. With his fleet, he controlled the all-important flow of commerce between Crete, the colonies, and other peoples; and this made him tremendously wealthy. Stone-lined vaults built underneath the palace overflowed with gold, silver, lapis lazuli, carnelian, and amethyst. Palaces and villas throughout Crete kept voluminous stocks of wine and olive oil, which were used for barter. The largest of these liquid treasuries was at Knossos, where storerooms on the ground floor of the palace held scores of huge clay jars with a total capacity exceeding 60,000 gallons. A cluster of small rooms lying beyond the storage area served as offices for the clerks who, scribbling their sums onto clay tablets, kept records of the goods available, of what was due their king, and of what he might owe to others. As in Sumer, it would seem that Crete's first writers were accountants.

For all their wealth and power, Minoan monarchs appear to have possessed a certain modesty. No stately monuments or sculptured effigies celebrate them. They built no imposing architectural memorials to themselves as did the Egyptian pharaohs. Paintings at the Knossos palace did not even hint at the rulers' achievements.

To administer their complex, trade-oriented society, Minoan kings relied on a many-layered hierarchy of provincial governors and officials. The higher posts in this bureaucracy were likely filled by members of the royal family. Some of the wealthy functionaries kept handsome villas in the country, where they supervised irrigation projects, vineyards, and olive orchards. Perhaps equally prominent in society and certainly essential to its welfare were the merchants and sea captains who took the country's produce abroad and returned with the profits. Some may have worked for the government, while others functioned as independent entrepreneurs. Those who grew wealthy in the import-export business built large homes in seacoast towns near the wharves where their ships unloaded luxury cargoes brought from abroad.

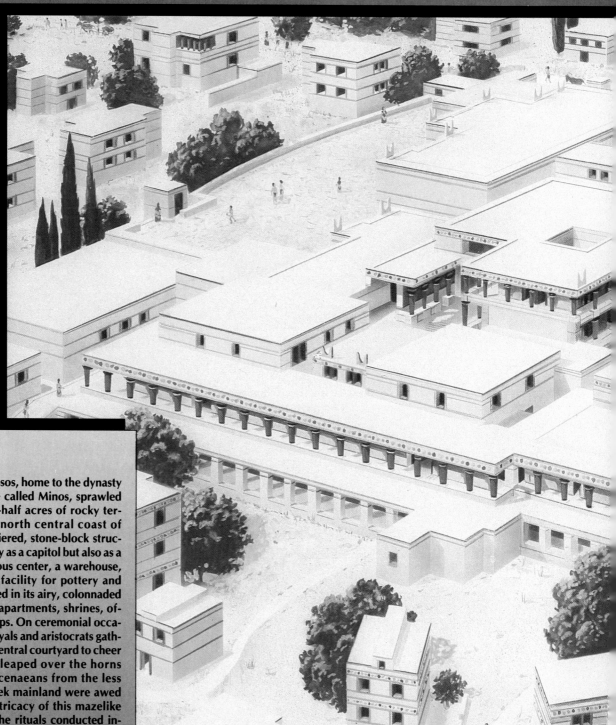

The palace at Knossos, home to the dynasty of kings who were called Minos, sprawled across four-and-a-half acres of rocky terrain close to the north central coast of Crete. The many-tiered, stone-block structure served not only as a capitol but also as a cultural and religious center, a warehouse, and a production facility for pottery and other crafts. Housed in its airy, colonnaded wings were royal apartments, shrines, offices, and workshops. On ceremonial occasions, crowds of royals and aristocrats gathered in the paved central courtyard to cheer acrobats as they leaped over the horns of wild bulls. Mycenaeans from the less sophisticated Greek mainland were awed by the size and intricacy of this mazelike structure and by the rituals conducted inside it. From their visits arose the legend of the great labyrinth, in which the beast called the Minotaur dwelled. The Mycenaean word *labyrs* referred to the double ax, which, as a sacred Minoan symbol, emblazoned walls and columns in the palace. The name *labyrinth* thus identified the Knossos palace as the "house of the double ax."

THE LABYRINTH OF MINOS

Crete's social ladder also included an aristocracy of nobles, priests, and priestesses; a middle class of artisans, artists, clerks, and lower-ranking officials; a proletariat of farmers, herders, and laborers; and an underclass of serfs. Despite the lowly nature of their status, serfs in Crete may have lived better than their counterparts in other early civilizations. The crude huts and the shanty-filled ghettos usually associated with slave systems did not exist in Cretan cities. Writing more than 1,000 years after the extinction of the Minoan culture, the Greek philosopher Aristotle claimed that Crete's serfs enjoyed the same privileges as other Minoan citizens with two notable exceptions: They were not allowed to bear arms and, curiously, they were forbidden to practice gymnastic exercises.

Although it continued to evolve and develop, Crete's social structure remained relatively stable over a period of many centuries. It revealed few signs of the discontent and upheaval that, from time to time, have wracked most cultures. Without a wall to protect them, the Minoan palaces were open to the teeming cities that surrounded them. The kings could not have survived a general rebellion, let alone a limited uprising. The tie that bound king to noble to merchant to artisan to farmer to serf was a strong one, perhaps a deeply rooted mutual dependency reinforced by the society's religious beliefs. Whatever the sources of its strength, Cretan society proved remarkably homogeneous and durable.

Homer's *Iliad* describes Crete as a bountiful land "densely peopled and boasting ninety cities" — no doubt a literary exaggeration. But during the Minoan golden age — 1700 to 1450 BC — the island's population apparently reached a quarter of a million. As many as 40,000 people may have lived in Knossos alone. Minoan artists had a penchant for crowd scenes and must have been familiar with urban throngs.

Most Minoans lived in cities and towns on or near the coast. Their two- and three-storied dwellings were jammed together along narrow streets that twisted out from the palaces or reached back from the wharves.

Wealthy citizens built residences with as many as a dozen rooms, while the less affluent made do with earth-floored bungalows of three rooms or less. Although some were oval shaped, most of the houses were rectangular and enclosed a central courtyard or patio. They usually were built on stone foundations and had stone rubble walls that were plastered with clay. Rooms were small and ceilings were low: The Cretans averaged only a bit more than five feet in height.

Both middle- and upper-class families lived comfortably, possibly better than their contemporaries in Egypt and Sumer. Their homes were well appointed, decorated on the outside in some cases with pots of flowers and even gardens. Inside their houses the Minoans sat and slept on furniture made from animal skins stretched over wooden frames. Neither homes nor palaces had fireplaces. For cooking and keeping warm in winter, the Minoans used portable clay or bronze braziers or fireboxes that burned wood. Dark interiors were lit with lamps made of clay, stone, or bronze and fueled by olive oil. Typical household implements included cooking pots that hung from tripods, ladles, funnels, and strainer jars for cheese making.

Minoans ate well. They made bread from wheat and barley flour, which they ground themselves in their homes. From fields and gardens they harvested lettuce, lentils, beans, peas, and squash. In sunny orchards they picked plums, quinces, and figs. The sea filled their baskets with octopus, clams, squid, and fish. Goats and cows provided the raw milk used to make cheese. In addition to wine, Cretans drank beer made from barley; many of their drinking jugs were ornamented with images of barley sprigs.

The highlighted symbol in this Minoan script — designated in modern times as Linear A — represents the word *wine*. Although Linear A has never been fully deciphered, the sample on the tablet probably documents a business transaction involving a quantity of wine. Writing developed on Crete much as it did earlier in Sumer and Egypt, with scribes making records of the transfer of goods from one owner to another. At first, scribes on Crete used pictographs, but in time, they developed a linear script in which stylized symbols represented the sounds of the spoken Minoan language.

Despite their fondness for good food, Minoans had an apparent horror of flabbiness. This is evident from their art. Men kept trim through gymnastics and other vigorous exercise, and they exaggerated their leanness with tight-fitting belts. They wore their hair long and usually went beardless. They favored simple loincloths or, for formal occasions, kilts and either sandals or boots. But the women, especially those of the royal court, were highly conscious of fashion. The women enhanced their slim figures with narrow-waisted skirts flounced in gaily colored tiers from hip to ankle. Above the waist they wore tight-fitting jackets that left the breasts bare. They often piled their dark hair high atop their heads in coiffures that sometimes included delicate ringlets that curved over the forehead and cheeks. Long tresses were held in place with ribbons or jewelry. To make themselves even more alluring, Minoan women reddened their lips, plucked their eyebrows with tweezers, and used eye shadow.

In general, the women of Crete seemed to have enjoyed far greater social freedom than their counterparts in other early civilizations, who were often treated as chattel. A fresco in the palace at Knossos depicts a crowd of stylish, extravagantly dressed women engaged in some sort of public festival. Their billowing hairdos fall over their shoulders and back, the tresses entwined in strings of jewels and beads. Engaged in lively conversation with a neighbor, one of the figures has extended one hand in what appears to be a gesture of feigned astonishment. The animated women, so obviously enjoying each other's company, seem anything but suppressed. In fact, women were free to mingle with men at public festivals. Cretan artists depicted women taking part in athletic events, holding the reins of chariots alongside the men. Women were equal in religion as well; in Minoan religious ceremonies, priestesses played prominent roles.

Minoan marriage rites appear to have been gentle and warm. An ivory engraving recovered near Knossos shows what seems to be a betrothal. The woman is barefoot and dressed in a flounced calf-length skirt and a bodice, and the man wears a loincloth with a dagger at his waist. The two face each other, holding hands with their arms bent at the elbow so that the forearms are almost touching. Another poignant scene is a fresco picturing a man standing behind a stylishly dressed woman, fastening a gold necklace around her throat.

Minoans probably celebrated their weddings much as they did any special occasion — with music and dance. They strummed, piped, and blew any number of instruments, including the stringed cithara, a kind of rattle called a sistrum, and the double pipes. Their music set the rhythm for a large assortment of both sacred and secular dances. It was once believed that Cretans invented dancing, and indeed, their artists often caught them in midstep. A terra-cotta piece excavated in eastern Crete shows a circle of three women with arms outstretched dancing around a fourth woman who is playing a cithara. On another artifact, the figures have joined hands and are moving in a slow, solemn rhythm similar to that of dances still done by the women of rural Crete. Theseus, the legendary Greek slayer of the Minotaur, was said to have witnessed Minoan women doing a "crane dance," which mirrored the movements of the water birds that strutted the island's marshes. In the *Iliad,* Homer describes a dance at ancient Knossos: "There were young men and young girls, sought for their beauty with gifts of oxen, dancing and holding hands at the wrist. The maidens wore long light robes, but the men wore tunics of finespun work shining softly, touched with olive oil. And the girls wore fair garlands on their heads, while the young men carried golden knives that hung from sword-belts of silver. At whiles on their understanding feet they would run very lightly, as when a potter crouching makes trial of his wheel, holding it close in his hands, to see if it will run smooth. At another time they would form rows and run, rows crossing each other. And around the lovely chorus of dancers stood a great multitude happily watching while among the dancers two acrobats led the measures of song and dance revolving around them."

In their quieter moments, Minoans enjoyed board games or went to theatrical entertainments. A gold-rimmed ivory board uncovered at Knossos may have been used to play a game similar to backgammon. At the palace in Phaistos, on Crete's southern coast, aristocrats played a game with pieces that resembled chessmen, some of them in the shape of a lion's head or carved to look like an ox's hoof. Also at Phaistos, people could attend special events at the palace arena. It had ten tiers for spectators rising around a flagstone courtyard that was employed as a stage. A similar arena at Knossos had eighteen rows of steps running up one side, six on the other, and in a corner, a private box for royalty.

The people of Crete earned their leisure and supported their prosperous lifestyles through hard work. Minoans exhibited consummate ability as engineers, builders, and masters of dozens of crafts. Gournia, an industrial town on the northeast coast, bustled with carpenters, weavers, metalsmiths, oil processors, and stonecutters who labored in their small homes. The carpenters worked with an extensive tool kit that included many implements whose form and function would not change much over the ensuing centuries — long and short saws, light and heavy chisels, awls, nails, files, and axes. A block of schist found in the home of one of Gournia's carpenters was used for casting metal tools. The mold was so precious to its owner that, when a jagged crack formed across the top, he repaired it with painstaking care. To close the crack, he bound the block with narrow strips of copper, tightening them by driving small stone wedges under the bands. In a room adjoining this carpentry shop, a number of stone and clay loom weights were found arranged in the order of their likely use.

From the Sumerians, metalworkers on Crete learned the secrets of making bronze. Foundries at Gournia and elsewhere on Crete produced the alloy by mixing imported tin with copper. The ore was melted in furnaces and then tipped into molds to harden. Minoan metalworkers were renowned for their skill. Smiths hammered sheets of bronze on an anvil, heated them at a fire, and joined them in layers to fashion spears, daggers, arrowheads, and largely ceremonial double axes. Soldiers all around the eastern Mediterranean prized Crete's excellent, rapier-like swords. Metal artisans also made fine jewelry, chains, and even locks; doors in the homes of wealthy Minoans contained sliding bronze pins that fit into holes in gypsum doorjambs.

The production of olive oil, the essential commodity for trade, was both an agricultural and an industrial task. To plant the saplings, Cretans turned the rocky island soil with a two-pronged plow. They irrigated some orchards with complex networks of canals and ditches. After the trees reached bearing age, usually in about four to five years, laborers knocked the fruit from the limbs with sticks and winnowed the olives from leaves with a rake or fork. Then they soaked the olives in hot water, crushed them in a press and deposited them in settling vats that were filled with water. After the oil rose to the surface, plugs were removed from spouts at the bottom of the vats to drain off the water.

Stonecutters at Gournia and elsewhere on the island sweated many hours in quarries to provide Crete's tireless builders with materials. Wielding picks, wedges, and augers, they hewed limestone, gypsum, and other native rock into square blocks for

ARTWORKS FOR CRETAN WALLS

The Minoans were among the earliest masters of fresco, the art of painting on plastered walls. This medium was the civilization's major art form: Interiors of villas and palaces on Crete were covered with fanciful impressions of life and nature in the seagirt Minoan world. Fresco artists were widely patronized by royalty and the wealthy.

A wall was prepared for painting with a thin layer of white lime plaster. Then, using an obsidian chip or other sharp instrument, the artist outlined the main features and sketched in important details. Next, the colors were applied, often while the surface was still moist so that they soaked in and made the painted images more durable.

A fresco from the throne room of the Knossos palace is reproduced below: Two griffins, beasts that were half eagle and half lion, crouched in a field of reeds and kept watch over the throne of the high priestess. On the following two pages are other examples of fresco art from Crete and also from Thera, an island colony where the Minoan artistic influence was strong.

A Minoan prince in a feathered bonnet

A monkey scrambling over rocks

African antelopes

A fisherman from the island of Thera

Children in a boxing match

Acrobats leaping a bull

A galley accompanied by playful dolphins

Courtly woman in a flounced skirt

A landscape with lilies and swallows

Priestess with offering

use as facing on palaces and grand houses. Serfs or free laborers lugged the stone into the towns and cities on crude, solid-wheeled carts. Since Minoans had no block and tackle, the heavy facing stones had to be loaded onto ramps and muscled up two or three stories to the top of walls under construction.

The paving of roads required enormous quantities of stone and labor. By late in the Minoan era, an extensive system of paved roads crisscrossed the island. Guardhouses were built at strategic intervals to ensure the free movement of travelers and their goods. Stone was also used in the building of bridges, causeways, and supports for the aqueducts that brought water to the cities and palaces.

The Minoans were expert at moving water — so much so that their feats of hydraulic engineering constitute one of their most impressive achievements. They built highly sophisticated aqueducts. At Knossos, a system of jointed earthenware pipes linked the palace with a mountain spring more than six miles away. The pipeline sections tapered so that one fit neatly into another. Stone bridges lifted the water over gulleys and ravines along the route.

For palace residents, the ample supply of fresh, running water made for a cleaner, more congenial life. They found dozens of imaginative ways to use it, surrounding themselves with fountains, pools, and streams. The bathing room at the palace at Phaistos was designed so that attendants could shower bathers from above. A small room in the queen's chambers at Knossos enclosed a toilet that could be flushed with water poured from a handy container.

Since Crete received torrential rains during the autumn and winter seasons, Minoan architects gave careful thought to drainage. In and around the Knossos palace, an intricate network of ducts, gutters, and basins funneled runoff into terra-cotta conduits so large that a man could stand comfortably inside them. A steep channel beside an outer stairway at Knossos presented a particularly challenging drainage problem. The staircase was broken into flights set at right angles. Unable to make the sharp turns, fast-flowing water would have poured out over the landings. To prevent flooding, engineers devised a way to slow the water by forcing it through a series of gently curving spouts.

Crete's artists were as meticulous and innovative as its architects and engineers. They imbued each of their creations — their sweeping wall murals, delicate pottery, handsome stone vases, exquisitely crafted jewelry, engraved seals, and carved ivory figurines with vitality and color. Demonstrating a distrust of the pretentious and the monumental, they avoided the geometric rigidity that was the hallmark of the contemporary art of the Egyptians and the Sumerians. Their work was distinguished as much by the artists' joyous appreciation of everyday experiences and the wonders of nature as by its careful crafting.

A marvelous piece of carved steatitic stone, named the "Harvester Vase" centuries after it was made, illustrates the Minoan style at its finest. Minoan artisans used chisels and drills to shape the vase and then hollowed it with an

Carved in black steatite, the bull's-head libation vessel at left, above, was employed as a container for sacred fluids. When the head was tilted forward, the liquid poured from the mouth. Bulls had a special religious significance for the Minoans, who placed giant stone bull's horns around their shrines and palaces to identify the areas as holy places. And during times of crisis, the Minoans followed the practice of sacrificing bulls on altars and offering their blood to the earth goddess.

abrasive powder. After carving a decorative scene on the exterior, they varnished it with oil. Striding two abreast around the vase, a group of peasants is shown heading for the fields in high spirits. With willow rakes thrown back on their shoulders, the figures appear to be laughing, shouting, or singing lustily. Walking with them is a musician in a skullcap who is waving a sistrum and leading a trio of singers. One peasant has fallen on the heels of the man in front of him, earning for himself a robust but good-natured reproach. In a similarly masterful life-size wall fresco, a Minoan artist lifts vivid detail from nature. A wildcat concealed in a thicket, head down and legs tensed, stalks a bird in a field blazing with flowers.

Frescoes had to be painted on wet plaster before it dried, a process that put a premium on speed and spontaneity. Artists concocted paints from such mineral substances as copper silicate (blue), carbonized wood (black), and ochre (red or yellow), and they used their colors freely. In depictions of human figures, which were invariably shown in profile, artists always painted the men red and the women white, a notion that probably was inspired by the Egyptians. They used other colors in similarly unrealistic ways; for example, vegetation was painted in a variety of colors — but rarely in green. In one fresco, a blue ape is shown among the beasts in a royal menagerie.

This same creative playfulness found its way into every form of Minoan art. Artisans fashioned bowls and vases with long spouts, sinuous handles, and rows of prickly

This tender tableau of a cow comforting her suckling calf reflects the Minoan artisans' fondness for depicting the natural world. The plaque was crafted of faience, a clay-like substance made by mixing ground quartz, potash, and water. The artisans fired their faience objects in a kiln, adding glazes to give the pieces a finish that was hard, shiny, and colorful.

studs. Metalworkers molded thin sheets of gold into the shapes of flowers, animals, and insects. The Minoans displayed a fondness for miniature artwork; they carved tiny scenes and geometric designs onto seals, gems, and beads. Some of the engravings were so minuscule that they could barely be seen with the naked eye.

Early in Crete's history, artists often inscribed cups, vases, seals, and other pieces of their artwork with a form of writing that apparently was employed by Minoan scribes as well. This script, incomprehensible to later generations, was based on a hieroglyphic alphabet that included symbols for people, animals, trees, tools, and other easily recognizable objects. After about 1700 BC, this limited form of writing gave way to a schematic script — the indecipherable Linear A — which was incised onto tablets of damp clay.

About three centuries later, a completely new set of written symbols appeared. Mostly used for accounting, this later script, which would be labeled Linear B, was adapted from the Greek language brought by Mycenaeans from the mainland. Unlike its predecessor, the Mycenaean script has been deciphered. A tablet found in the palace armory at Knossos apparently was part of an inventory list and reads as follows: "Horse-vehicle, painted red, with bodywork fitted, supplied with reins; the rail of wild fig-wood with jointing of horn. . . . One chariot."

The early Minoan alphabet may have been taught to apprentice clerks or to children in classrooms. Tablets found on stone benches lining the walls of a small room near the royal suite at Knossos were used for writing practice. At the top of each tablet, a sentence was written out in a firm hand, probably by a teacher. In the space below, students made shaky attempts to duplicate it.

The Minoans worshipped nature. Some images on vases, rings, seals, and frescoes depict people in attitudes of reverence before objects in the natural world — mountains, trees, birds, snakes, and bulls. Because they considered all things and all places to be sacred, Minos and his people erected few temples and no great religious monuments. Instead, they kept simple, private shrines in their homes and worshipped in forests, on mountaintops, or in one of the many caves carved into the limestone landscape of Crete by dripping water. In the mouths of these caves, Minoans left homemade offerings — clay and bronze figurines, knives and swords, or pottery and seals — in the hope that they might please the spirits of both this world and the netherworld. At Knossos, the gloomy, cavelike palace basement served as a place of worship for the royal family.

Even though the Minoans believed devoutly in the afterlife, they made no special effort to preserve the remains of the dead. Early in their cultural evolution they built collective tombs called *tholos,* low, round stone structures that may have had vaulted roofs. Other tombs were constructed on a rectangular plan, as if to imitate the houses of the living. Regardless of the form, it appears that the Minoans may have simply buried their dead in the ground and at some later date transferred the bones to the tombs. These structures were used for centuries by large families and clans; periodically, the tombs were cleaned out and a fresh earthen floor was laid down in preparation for another cycle of burial. Like caves and other dark places, tombs were thought to be passages to the netherworld, and they were often furnished with ordinary

Of all the Minoan religious symbols, the double ax was the holiest. Stylized axes such as this gold miniature consecrated shrines in Cretan homes and palaces. Full-size double axes were used by priests to kill sacrificial bulls in ceremonies to propitiate the mother goddess.

In this faience statue, the mother goddess of Crete wears the flounced skirt and open bodice of a courtly Minoan woman. The dove perched on her head marked her as divine, while the snakes writhing in her grip reminded the faithful of her close ties to the mysterious underworld. The goddess was the essence of Minoan religion. Her spirit imbued everything in the natural world: earth, air, trees, and stones — even the palace pillars.

domestic articles to help the deceased set up housekeeping in their next life.

A deity of great significance for the Minoans was the mother goddess, whose likeness appeared on countless art objects. Early in the evolution of Minoan civilization, she was pictured as plump and matronly. But later she was shown as an elegant Minoan woman dressed in flounced skirt and open-breasted jacket.

At times, the mother goddess appeared with a young man who may have represented her son, a lesser deity worshipped perhaps as the personification of seasonal death and rebirth of nature. In a later era, the Greeks would believe that this Cretan had been the principal Greek god, Zeus, as a boy.

Sometimes the mother goddess was shown with snakes rearing from her hands or draped around her body. The snakes were not necessarily considered threatening; rather, they were benevolent visitors from the netherworld who guarded houses and the families who lived in them against a variety of evils. But the power of the mother goddess herself extended far beyond the home. She ruled supreme over humankind and nature; she could influence harvests, the weather, and many other forces over which the people of Crete had little or no control themselves. Her divine powers were invoked through offerings, dance, and prayer. Minoans prayed by raising the right hand with the palm facing forward and the fingers spread or by placing the right hand on the forehead.

Like dance and prayer, athletic competition was considered to be a form of worship. To honor the mother goddess and Crete's other deities, athletes competed in running, jumping, wrestling, and boxing. Protected to a degree by gloves, helmets, and leather leggings, the fighters used both fists and feet to thrash each other in boxing matches. The intensity of this sort of action is demonstrated on a Minoan stone carving that re-creates three boxing scenes. In the first depiction, a fighter cocks a gloved fist above his prostrate opponent; in the second, two boxers are exchanging blows and one of them is about to go down; the third shows a pair of combatants on their backs but still fighting it out with their feet.

The most popular — and dangerous — Minoan athletic event was bull-leaping, an acrobatic spectacle in which daredevils toyed with charging bulls. Risking life and limb on their agility, the acrobats would grasp the horns of the onrushing bull and somersault — or be thrown — over the animal's head. Some leapers did a handstand on the animal's back while others landed feet first before somersaulting into the arms of a companion. Wild bulls were captured and trained for these exhibitions. A gold cup of Minoan design shows a bull cozying up to a decoy cow while a quick-handed Cretan tethers one of the bull's hind legs. To develop the precise timing required for a performance, bull-leapers practiced with tame bulls. To face a wild bull in the arena, they needed great courage as well as skill; no doubt, athletes were often killed while attempting a jump. In a breathtaking fresco at Knossos, a poised female acrobat has grabbed the horns of an enormous bull; an airborne male figure is already in the midst of a tremendous vaulting leap over the bull, pushing off from its back with his hands. A second female figure stands behind the bull, waiting with arms outstretched to guide the jumper's descent.

Bull-leaping entertained crowds on Crete for more than five hundred years, but it had greater significance than being an exhilarating stunt. The spectacle was a sacred ritual observed in honor of the mother goddess. And a crucial act of this holy drama came after the performance, when the bull was sacrificed in the name of the goddess.

Because the Minoans considered all elements of the natural world to be holy, they worshipped almost anywhere, in rude caves and basements and in lofty sanctuaries such as this cloud-swept shrine in eastern Crete. Rising from a craggy outcropping of rock at the summit of a mountain, the shrine attracted processions of pilgrims, who brought offerings to honor the mother goddess. The stylized horns set atop the cornices mark the place as a holy precinct.

Doubtless through such blood sacrifices the Minoans hoped to appease the goddess and enlist her aid in averting a host of disasters: shipwreck, accidents, disease, failed crops — and particularly earthquakes. Earthquakes victimized the Minoans regularly, striking with savage force perhaps as often as twice a century and in milder seizures much more frequently. The results could be calamitous: Houses, palaces, even whole towns were destroyed and many citizens killed, crushed in the stone rubble. The threat of such earthborne violence was never far from the Cretan consciousness. It is possible that the Minoans associated earthquakes with a bull-god who dwelt beneath the ground, that in the muffled roar of the shaking earth they heard the bellow of the beast and thought that their world was being tossed on the bull-god's horns. Such a belief might account for the ritual sacrifice of bulls.

The Minoans petitioned their gods in other ways to prevent such catastrophes. The residents of the Knossos palace worshipped the pillars that underpinned the building. To give the pillars additional strength, the Minoans consecrated them by painting on one of their culture's oldest and holiest symbols, the double ax.

In the end, no amount of supplication availed. Early in the fifteenth century BC, a series of quakes and aftershocks swept across Crete, causing great destruction and loss of life. Perhaps because of the dismay of the people, internal conflict further disrupted Crete's serenity. Fighting broke out between the dynasty of Knossos and the other rulers around the island. Eventually the kingdom of Knossos emerged as victor, and all the other palaces were destroyed. But the internal upheaval had weakened Crete and made it vulnerable — a fact that did not go unrecognized by the bellicose Mycenaeans of the Greek mainland.

The Mycenaeans, who may have learned their seamanship from the Minoans, moved quickly to take advantage of the temporary Minoan weakness, seizing a number of the Minoan island colonies. Repeated attempts by the Mycenaeans to capture Crete itself were thwarted until, about 1450 BC, another natural disaster intervened to help the attackers — and sounded the death knell for the Minoan culture.

This time the catastrophe was a volcanic eruption on the island of Thera, just seventy miles north of Crete. The volcano exploded with such force that it created a tidal wave as high as 200 feet and sent it hurtling down on the Minoan homeland. Doubtless this wall of water wiped out harbor installations and killed thousands in the cities on Crete's heavily populated north coast. It may have swamped and wrecked the entire Minoan fleet, leaving the island all but defenseless.

It was not long before Knossos and the rest of Crete fell to the Greeks, along with the remaining Minoan colonies in the Aegean. By 1400 BC, the survivors of the upheaval were scattered in isolated pastoral settlements. The palace at Knossos was occupied; inventory tablets for the stores there were being written in a form of Greek. New palace frescoes were being painted in a stiff, symmetrical style that would have been alien to the more spontaneous Minoan artists. Then the palace itself was destroyed; its end came suddenly, in a storm of fire and collapsing masonry. The sparkling era of the Minoans had slipped into the shadows.

EUROPE'S SACRED MEGALITHS

In western Europe, thousands of miles from the first centers of civilization, human muscle and imagination produced a collection of structures as remarkable in their way as Egypt's pyramids or Mesopotamia's ziggurats. These eerie monuments, consisting of great mounds and complex arrangements of massive boulders, came to be known as megaliths — from the Greek words *megas* and *lithos,* or "great stone." Their builders were the Stone Age villagers of Europe, an intermixture of primitive hunter-gatherers and farmers who migrated from regions that lay to the east beginning about 6000 BC. These early Europeans could not write, and thus they left behind no records. And they lacked other important attributes of civilized life: They built no cities, framed no laws, and formed no states. But as the megaliths demonstrate, they were amazingly industrious and ingenious engineers. A total of nearly 50,000 megaliths, large and small, continue to dot the European landscape. Some of their component stones weigh fifty tons and more, yet they were maneuvered into position using only crude ropes and logs as rollers.

The structures were erected on the island of Malta, in Spain and Portugal, in many

areas of France and the British Isles, and as far to the north as Denmark. Some of them were large underground communal tombs that, after being constructed of stones or cut from living rock, were covered over with earth and sod.

Others were built above ground and consisted of upright stones. These open-air monuments were long believed to have been shrines of some sort. Recently, mathematicians have demonstrated that several also functioned as observatories, their stones giving the learned men of the villages sight lines on the heavenly bodies. At one such structure, England's Stonehenge, observers could determine the longest day of the year by noting when the sun rose over the tip of a certain outlying stone. Applying this knowledge, the people could then figure out the length of the year and devise a calendar.

The megaliths were erected over a span of 3,000 years. And since the earliest of the monuments predate the building of Egypt's pyramids, the Stone Age farmers of Europe rank as the first humans to raise structures intended to last forever.

Its huge stones throwing long shadows in a winter sunset, Stonehenge dominates southern England's Salisbury Plain. The monument was built in stages over a period of 1,500 years — a span of fifty generations. First, a circular trench was dug by villagers with crude tools of stone and bone about 2750 BC. Some decades later, other teams of workers elaborated the shrine, erecting an inner horseshoe of great boulders — called trilithons — that weighed an average of twenty-six tons each. Around this horseshoe rose a ring of other stones topped with a continuous lintel. The ring's massive sarsens, as they are known, were quarried twenty miles away and dragged overland to the site. On the circumference of the trench, a pair of slabs formed an entrance. Aligned with this portal was the important "heel stone" *(lower left)* over which the sun rose at the summer solstice.

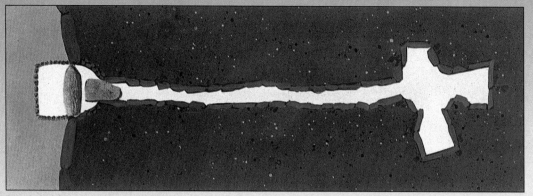

Overview of the passage grave at New Grange showing cruciform floor plan.

Under a covering of dirt and sod, the stones of the great Irish tomb called New Grange, completed about 3100 BC, demonstrate the builders' extraordinary skills. The slabs that form the roof of the high, narrow main passageway were laid to make an arch that has remained intact for 5,000 years. In addition, a gap in the front of the passage is so precisely angled that shortly after dawn on the day of the winter solstice — and at no other time — a shaft of sunlight shines down the passage's entire length, illuminating the back of the chamber in the center of the mound.

One of the largest of all the Maltese megalithic temples, this structure on the island of Gozo came to be known locally as *Ggantija,* or "gigantic." It is two temples in one. The main three-chambered and cloverleaf-shaped shrine measures 100 feet across, from the entrance to the back court.

STIRRINGS IN ASIA

As the first great civilizations took shape in the sun-drenched river basins of Mesopotamia and Egypt, a similar impulse began to stir in three widely separated regions many thousands of miles to the east. Small bands of wandering tribespeople — some hunters and gatherers, others nomadic herders — settled down to till the soil. Then, as though following a shared instinct too deep to articulate, they each began to create their own form of civilized life.

One such transformation took place in the floodplain of the Indus River, in present-day Pakistan. Sometime around 2500 BC, a people of unknown origin started constructing a series of cities, as remarkable as any the world had yet seen. Artisans set to work, trade flourished, and a system of writing evolved. At its apogee, the Indus civilization encompassed nearly half a million square miles; its boundaries stretched from the foothills of the Himalayas to the Arabian Sea and from the Ganges watershed to the Gulf of Cambay, just to the north of what is now Bombay. It was the largest cultural domain of its era.

Another transformation took place in the lowlands of Southeast Asia, where groups of anonymous farmers, living in small, apparently independent villages, devised a method of cultivating rice, the future staple grain of all southern Asia. This people also perfected the art of casting objects in bronze, a breakthrough in technology that ranks among humankind's greatest early achievements.

Then, in the vast and fertile expanses of northern China, along the banks of the Yellow River, a third Asian civilization began to emerge. Here the inhabitants grew and harvested millet, raised pigs, and wove silk. Artisans among them turned out vessels of pottery, and later of bronze, whose elegance and craftsmanship would never be surpassed. Theirs was a culture so stable and so self-sufficient that it has continued unbroken to this day.

The full story of the development of each of these civilizations remains tantalizingly elusive. Their histories are a blend of fact and conjecture because scholars have no understandable written languages to use as a guide. The pictographic script of the Indus people has not yet been successfully deciphered. The southeast Asian rice farmers seem not to have developed a system of writing. And while ancient Chinese chronicles recount the lives and exploits of a succession of dynastic rulers that extends back to the twenty-fourth century BC, the only surviving scrolls date from more than 2,000 years after that time. How much is fact, and how much reverent fabrication, may never be determined. Nevertheless, the general outlines of these civilizations are clear. In the Indus Valley, the legacy is particularly striking.

The earliest known inhabitants along the Indus River were nomadic herders from the hills of Baluchistan, not far to the west. At first, their stay in the valley was dictated by the seasons. Each year, harsh highland winters would drive them to lower ground, where they could fatten their herds of sheep and goats on the lush valley grasses. Then, as summer approached and a hot sun began beating down on the land, the herders would return to the cool hills.

In the middle of the fourth millennium BC, the pattern began to change. Some families, besides tending their flocks, planted small garden plots — patches of barley and wheat that they worked with stone tools and watered with animal-skin buckets that they filled at the river. They harvested the plots in the spring before they began their trek back to the Baluchistan heights. As time went on, some clans settled in the valley for the summer as well. Gradually, the temporary grazing stations gave way to year-round farming villages.

Compared with the rugged Baluchistan heights, the Indus Valley countryside was inviting and productive. Broad sweeps of grassland alternated with expanses of timber — cedar, teak, rosewood, tamarisk, and acacia. The climate was moist and mild. The southwest monsoon probably passed over parts of the region, bringing a season of summer rainfall.

Wildlife abounded. Herds of elephants, antelopes, rhinoceroses, and wild hogs roamed the grassy savannahs. Tigers and leopards prowled the forests, preying on deer and peafowl. There were bears and wolves, parrots and eagles, monkeys, squirrels, tortoises, and mongooses. The marshes along the riverbanks were home to water buffaloes and crocodiles, as well as all kinds of water birds. The river teemed with many species of fish.

Just as in Sumer and Egypt, the river's most bounteous gift to the people who settled in the valley was an annual flood. Each spring, as snows melted in the Himalayas, the Indus would spill over its banks, covering the land with sediment that would serve as a natural fertilizer for the crops.

Scores of farm settlements came to dot the Indus plains and the valleys that pushed like fingers into the surrounding foothills. One site, at Amri on the river's lower reaches, took shape in the middle of the fourth millennium BC and grew into a village encompassing twenty acres. Its inhabitants built small, rectangular dwellings of mud brick with roofs of mud-plastered thatch and with cellars for storage. Amri artisans used the potter's wheel to craft a variety of earthenware vessels, which they decorated with black geometric designs. They fashioned beads and trinkets from terra-cotta and shell. Most tools were made of wood or stone — though a few fortunate villagers might have wielded copper implements. Farmers used slingshots with stone missiles to drive pests and predators from their fields and pastures.

The Amri people belonged to a single tribal group that embraced some twenty neighboring villages. Other tribes settled to the north along the upper Indus beside various tributaries that forked into the Punjab region; they too depended on the silt deposits of annual flooding.

It was a precarious existence for all. The Indus, despite its beneficence, was also a source of grave danger. The yearly flood could sweep over a vast territory and force people to abandon their villages. Sporadically, the river would shift its course, inundating new stretches of land and depriving other areas. But by the middle of the third millennium, the Indus people had learned to deal with the river's vagaries. They brought most of the alluvial plain under cultivation and began to produce surplus crops, which became the basis for social organization. In time, they built grand cities, centers of production and trade.

One of these cities began modestly as a village on the banks of the Ravi, a major

Indus tributary in eastern Punjab. It came to be known as Harappa, and it gave the civilization its name.

The Harappans wisely declined to try to tame the Indus — they must have realized that such a conquest was manifestly impossible, although they did build strong levees and complex irrigation systems. The great secret of their civilization was in learning to rise above the river's floodwaters. In the same way the Sumerians had founded some of their cities — Ur among them — the Harappans erected their metropolises on immense mounds of earth and rubble, manmade islands safely out of danger on the broad plains. Among the first structures at Harappa was a huge citadel nearly 1,400 feet long and 600 feet wide, sitting alongside the Ravi on a plateau forty feet above the floodplain. To shield this edifice from erosion by the floodwaters, Harappan architects faced the foundation with a brick embankment forty-five feet thick at the base. And to protect the citadel from invaders, they built a sturdy wall atop the embankment and enforced it with towers and battlements.

Directly to the north of the citadel, the Harappan builders erected another, slightly smaller platform. On this foundation they constructed what might have been brick granaries, threshing floors, barracks for laborers, and loading platforms for grain.

By 2500 BC, civilizations were burgeoning in three disparate regions of the Far East. On the banks of the Indus River and its tributaries, a disciplined people known as the Harappans were practicing irrigation and laying out cities. In Southeast Asia, near the Mekong River, rice cultivation fostered the growth of large villages, where metalworkers and other artisans attained a high degree of skill. Along the Yellow River in China, the activities of farmers, artisans, merchants, and aristocrats intertwined to form the first strands of a great social fabric.

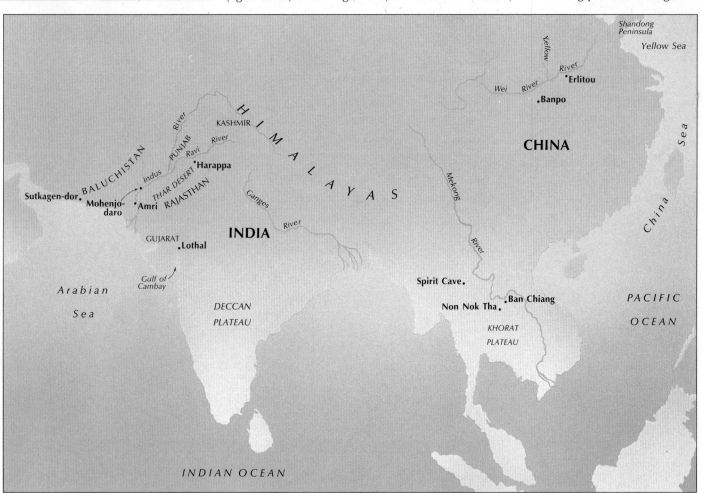

131

There was also a set of furnaces, which were used, in part, for forging bronze.

The entire complex, including the citadel and the granary areas, had a circumference of more than three miles. At the height of its civilization, around 2300 BC, Harappa was home to 35,000 people.

Another great city took shape 350 miles to the south, on the lower Indus. It was so nearly identical to the city of Harappa in size and configuration that it might have been laid out by the same master architect. Centuries later it was given the name Mohenjo-daro — "Hill of the Dead," in Sindhi. But in the third millennium, it was swarming with industrious life. From the plain, its citadel was reached by a ramp and ceremonial terraces. Two gateways permitted access through the wall. Within were assembly halls, administrative offices, and a number of residences for various officials and functionaries.

Only an enormous collective effort could have created these two great urban cen-

Oxen haul a cart laden with jars of grain along a thriving commercial thoroughfare in the Harappan city of Mohenjo-daro. At harvest time, wheat and barley were transported from outlying fields to the city granary to be distributed during the year to the residents. Among the recipients were officials who administered Mohenjo-daro's affairs, potters who crafted the vessels for the grain and other perishables, and weavers who fashioned garments of soft cotton, which was first grown here in the Indus Valley.

ters of the Indus culture. Thousands of laborers were needed to raise the platforms on which the buildings stood and to produce the brick that faced their walls. Thousands more had to work the fields to provide the agricultural surplus that such enterprises required. To direct this activity, there had to be a large and sophisticated bureaucracy of engineers, supervisors, and accountants. And in each of these cities, a powerful and imaginative central authority must have resided.

Whether a still-higher authority directed the entire Indus Valley culture has never been determined. But the remarkable uniformity of the twin cities — and of countless lesser sites scattered throughout the Indus Valley — suggests that strong lines of communication were responsible for shaping the experience of the Indus people. Most settlements in the ancient world appear to have grown up haphazardly, with winding streets that might have started as footpaths and with structures placed largely according to the builder's whim. But in the Indus culture, each town and city seems to have been laid out according to a pattern: a west-facing citadel, surrounded by housing blocks and intersected with a north-south gridwork of major thoroughfares. While numerous alleyways sliced randomly through the individual housing sections, the principal streets ran as straight as spear shafts.

Even the bricks were uniform. The Indus people built with two types: They used fired brick for foundation work and for the walls of important civic structures and a sun-dried brick that went into landfill and into the walls of private houses.

Indus houses, all similar in design, were built for durability and privacy. Family life centered around an interior courtyard, where meals were cooked and eaten. A number of small rooms and passageways — sleeping quarters, storage cubicles, and the like — surrounded the courtyard. The rooms, plastered in mud and gypsum, were sparsely furnished; family members reclined on reed mats or sat on low stools of wood or woven reeds.

Exterior walls presented a stark face unrelieved by windows. The main entrance to each dwelling opened on one of the narrow, dog-leg lanes that angled through the housing block. There was no attempt at external display — no grand entrances, no stately façades. And while individual dwellings ranged in size from two or three rooms to several dozen, the prosperous families apparently lived not much differently from their more modest neighbors.

One luxury that all Indus people shared was rare in the ancient world: indoor plumbing. Each house had a bathroom with a paved sloping floor and a brick drainpipe. The bath water was hauled by bucket from brick-lined wells, many of which were built into the houses themselves. There were no bathtubs; the people preferred to douse themselves from hand-held pitchers. But they did use toilets, which consisted of brick seats placed over narrow channels that led to drains.

The outflow from the houses went into an ingenious municipal sewage system. A covered cesspit outside each dwelling was designed to overflow into a network of brick-lined sewage channels. The channels, paved over in brick or stone tile, ran beside the major streets. There was a sump at each intersection, with a removable cover to permit cleaning. A corps of municipal sanitation workers must have been employed full time, not only tending this system, but also collecting refuse from the trash chutes that stretched from each residence to a bin in the street.

As in other early civilizations, home was workplace as well as dwelling for some citizens. A number of houses contained shops where family members might weave and dye cloth, throw pottery, or hammer out bowls and implements of copper. But the main source of prosperity was agriculture — and the city administrators devoted close attention to the organization and development of farming.

The huge complexes at Mohenjo-daro and Harappa that are believed to be municipal granaries covered thousands upon thousands of square feet. They had raised brick floors, which would have allowed air to circulate underneath — thus keeping the grain from mildewing — and strong, timbered roofs to protect against the weather. The apparent threshing areas nearby were paved in brick and included circular pits where workers pounded the kernels with wooden staves to remove the husks. Adjoining barracks provided housing for the labor force; each worker was accorded a small, two-room apartment.

The harvest was most likely a state monopoly, and the granaries served, in effect, as state treasuries. Wheat and barley were the staple crops, planted in autumn as the floods receded, then harvested the following spring. But as farming methods improved and a system of levees and irrigation ditches gave increasing control over the water supply, the people learned to cultivate a variety of crops throughout the year. Citizens might supplement their diet with peas, pomegranates, melons, dates, and other vegetables and fruit. Millet and sorghum came into favor as summer crops. Sesame, originally imported from Africa, was harvested for its seeds, which were pressed in order to extract oil for cooking.

Most of these crops were widespread throughout the ancient world, but the Indus people achieved one important agricultural breakthrough. They were the world's first people to grow cotton and to weave its fibers into textiles. Cotton breechcloths and dyed cotton cloaks became standard dress in the Indus Valley.

Indus farmers also raised a variety of domestic animals. Sheep and goats, first brought to the valley by tribal herders, provided meat, wool, and possibly milk. The grassy countryside was a natural range for cattle, and the farmers had several breeds, including the humpbacked zebu. Chicken, ducks, and pigeons were raised as well. The region's wild pigs were trapped and domesticated. The water buffalo was pressed into service as a draft animal, along with the elephant. There were also donkeys and, in desert areas, a few camels, which were probably imported from the Middle East.

These people revered animals. They painted them on pottery, carved their likenesses into statuettes and bas-reliefs, and brought them into their homes as pets. A family might keep a caged parrot, or perhaps a monkey. Children played with terra-cotta whistles in the shapes of hens. Ceramic monkeys that danced on strings were also popular toys; the string was threaded through a curved notch in the body so that the monkey could slide down smoothly when the string was held slack but would jerk to a halt when the string was pulled tight. When this game grew boring, a youngster might turn to a collection of ceramic bulls with heads that wiggled; the bulls could be hitched to two-wheeled toy carts like the ones the elders used to haul grain.

A number of craft industries added to the valley's prosperity. Aside from the work that went on in the home, groups of artisans would collect in manufacturing zones at the edge of town to pursue their trades. Toolmakers produced knives, hammers, axes, drills, cleavers, swords, and arrowheads. Most of the heavy implements were fashioned either from stone or from bone or wood. Copper was shaped into knives and razors; but bronze was rare, since one basic ingredient, tin, had to be imported from far outside the valley. Although many of these implements were weapons, they seem to have been used more frequently for hunting than for conquest or defense. The Indus Valley people appear to have been generally peaceful.

Potters threw a large assortment of vessels, some mass-produced for everyday use and others painstakingly embellished with artful black-on-red designs reminiscent of those made by earlier artisans from Amri. There were cooking pots, serving plates, water jugs, storage vats, cosmetic jars. So many shattered drinking cups were left about that guests at banquets must have flung them to the ground after imbibing, a lusty tradition that sprang up in many cultures.

The potters' repertory included much more than crockery. They made ceramic writing sticks, terra-cotta back scrubbers, dice and game markers of glazed earthenware, as well as pottery animal cages and, it seems, mousetraps. The potters turned out ceramic children's toys, which often were crudely made, and animal figurines that were masterpieces of close observation and meticulous craftsmanship and clearly intended for display.

The Indus city dwellers were fond of adorning themselves in trinkets and bangles, and a sizable jewelry industry evolved. A rich merchant or government official might wear an inlaid gold plaque at his chest or a golden armband or headband. Women favored necklaces and bracelets, beaded girdles, and elaborate hairdos fastened with combs, gold pins, or beaded fillets. Particularly dazzling were cone-shaped ornaments that fit over the ears like golden ear muffs.

Indus beadmakers produced their wares in an enormous variety of shapes, sizes, and materials, from gold to silver to common clay. And they imported quantities of semi-precious stones — jade from the Himalayas, lapis lazuli from Afghanistan, turquoise from Persia, amethysts from the Indian Deccan Plateau, bloodstone and jasper from India's Rajasthan region. A common material was steatite, a soapstone found in Baluchistan, which jewelers either made into beads or ground into a paste and fired in a kiln to create small baubles of faience. Decorative and cheap, these products of the Indus bead shops found their way to cities throughout the Middle East, and may well have been a major item in the valley's thriving export trade.

An instinct for commerce ran deep in the Indus people. Local merchants bartered from city to city, transporting their goods along the river in barges or overland in pack trains. Gradually, they extended their routes to alien lands.

One of their major exports was certainly the cotton that the Indus people alone knew how to grow at the time, as well as the brightly dyed textiles they wove from its fibers. Timber was another likely export, including cedar from the Kashmir region to the northeast and teak from the forests of the Punjab. The exporters also carried ivory, gemstones, and possibly spices, along with the ubiquitous bangles and baubles. Caravans fanned out through Baluchistan to bring back steatite, as well as alabaster and a tarry bitumen that was used for waterproofing. Farther north, Afghanistan provided gold, silver, and perhaps tin. The trails extended through Persia to the Caspian Sea and into Asia Minor.

Trading posts were established far beyond the valley's fringes. The Indus people founded a settlement at Sutkagen-dor, west of Baluchistan and within reach of the Persian Gulf. To the south of the valley, a large seaport took shape at Lothal on the Gulf of Cambay, with some of the most sophisticated port facilities of the era. The architects constructed a warehouse and docking complex of halved bricks with a large, rectangular boat basin equipped with a sluice gate to regulate the water level; it may have been the earliest enclosure built for ships. From Lothal, high-prowed, double-ended sailing vessels carried the gold, gems, and timber products of southern India along the coast to the Indus Valley and beyond.

One of the two great centers of Harappan culture, the carefully planned city of Mohenjo-daro was divided by a corridor more than 200 yards wide. A natural channel of the Indus River, or a canal leading to the river, may once have coursed through this open space, emphasizing the separation of the city's two sections.

Most of the population lived east of the corridor *(background, left)* in brick houses, some with floor plans so similar they seem to have been designed by the same architect. Dwellings had stark, windowless exteriors and opened onto narrow alleys rather than onto the busy main streets.

West of the corridor, a mound of mud brick and rubble lifted a number of large public buildings more than twenty feet above the Indus River floodplain. Those who built the ritual bath, adjacent granary, assembly halls and other edifices atop the mound devoted very little effort to external decoration; unlike the architects of other early civilizations, the Harappans built no lofty colonnades, no ornate façades.

A WELL-ORDERED CITY

The richest trade route from the valley lay to the west, through the Persian Gulf to Mesopotamia. Starting around 2350 BC, traffic with the urban centers of Sumer and Akkad expanded to become a prime source of revenue. Indus merchants settled in overseas colonies to trade with the Mesopotamians, and with their king, Sargon, who was much enamored of foreign goods.

The tight organization that characterized Indus cities was evident in their commerce. How much overseas trade was state controlled, and how much private enterprise, is not known. But all negotiations, domestic or foreign, were carried out according to precise standards. Merchants used sets of cubical stone weights that never varied in value throughout the Indus region. The basic unit was 16, equal to one-half ounce. The larger weights were multiples of 16 — 32, 64, 128, and so on up to 12,800 (twenty-five pounds); the smaller ones were all fractions of 16. The same ratio survives today in Indian money; 16 annas equal one rupee.

Measurements of length were also standardized throughout the culture. The Harappans used two systems: a "foot" of 13.2 inches, and a cubit of 20.62 inches. Everywhere in the valley, the people followed one of these two units of measure, whether building a house, surveying a field, or running out a length of fabric.

The Indus merchants, like their Sumerian counterparts, developed a method of recordkeeping and used carved stone seals to stamp their property. Every mercantile family had its own device, and probably every important citizen did also. More than 2,000 examples have been found in the Indus cities, and others have turned up in Mesopotamia, left there by overseas traders. Cut from steatite, and square or rectangular in shape with a loop on the back for threading on a necklace or wristband, the seals generally depict animals such as bulls, buffaloes, goats, and elephants. One popular motif appears to have been a unicorn sniffing at an incense burner. The unicorn is probably a bull shown in profile, so that one horn hides the other. But why the creature has been offered incense is a puzzlement. In a seal from Mohenjo-daro, both the unicorn and the incense brazier are being carried aloft in some kind of procession. The occasion might be a folk celebration or a solemn religious rite.

Another scene portrays a man in a tree leaning down toward a tiger, as if to hand the beast something. Yet another depicts a monster with the head of a man, the trunk and tusks of an elephant, the horns of a bull, and the hindquarters of a tiger. The meaning of these images can only be guessed at.

Compounding the mystery, each seal bears a written inscription in pictographic characters that have resisted interpretation. While some symbols are clear enough — a wheel, or a fish — others are abstract forms. The scribes used about 250 such signs, along with various modifying strokes, in a manner suggesting that each one stood for a syllable of the spoken language. But the Indus tongue is lost to antiquity, and none of the signs corresponds to any used by the Egyptians or the Sumerians.

The seal inscriptions are brief — one or two lines. Most likely they represented the owner's name or family motto, or perhaps a quotation from some ritual of worship. Any lengthier writings have long since disappeared. The Indus people left no surviving histories, no religious texts, no literary epics.

Such works must once have existed, however, for the Indus script could only have evolved from a well-established tradition. Accountants in the citadels would have recorded the amounts of wheat and barley collected as well as the exports and imports. Scribes would also have helped to devise a calendar, essential for predicting the annual Indus floods and for determining when to begin the planting season. The complex uniformity of Indus city life itself suggests that there was an efficient bureaucracy of scribal administrators.

The reigning intelligence that controlled the Indus civilization remains another mystery. The priesthood probably played a prominent role, as it did in Sumer and Egypt. But whether the priesthood ruled supreme or served as adviser to a line of potentates has not been determined. The chief authority could even have resided in a civic council of merchants, artisans, and landowners. The evidence is lacking, for the Harappans built no palaces, nor any large temples in the manner of the Sumerians and the Egyptians. Even the seat of government remains in doubt. Mohenjo-daro and Harappa were so nearly identical in size and configuration that either one could have qualified. Perhaps they ruled jointly.

Harappan religion is another matter for conjecture. The valley's first inhabitants worshipped a mother goddess, similar in many ways to the matronly fertility beings revered in the Middle East and Europe. Tribespeople in Baluchistan and in the Indus Valley fashioned crude terra-cotta statuettes and adorned them with necklaces and elaborate headdresses in the shape of fans. These effigies were paid homage in household shrines — a practice that continued into Harappan times and survives today in rustic Indian villages.

As Harappan religion evolved, various animals came to be regarded as sacred, including the unicorn found on the signature seals and the monstrous minotaurs — creatures that were half human and half animal. Foremost among the holy beasts was the humpbacked zebu. In addition, the fig tree, or pipal, seems to have been an object of veneration: Such a tree appears on seals, with a horned deity perched in its branches and female devotees surrounding it. Harappan belief may also have included a cult of hero worship similar to that practiced in Mesopotamia, for one seal displays a muscular person grappling with two tigers — a motif reminiscent of the Sumerian hero Gilgamesh.

The chief Harappan deity may well have been a horned, many-faced figure that was found on many seals, attended by his court of animals. In some renditions, he sits on a stool; in others, he sits in the traditional posture of a yogi, or Indian holy man, with his legs bent double and heels touching. While only three of his faces show, he may have been conceived by the Harappans as having four, so that he could look out simultaneously in all four directions. His four largest animal associates — elephant, tiger, buffalo, and rhinoceros — may have symbolized the four points of the compass. Moreover, in one seal, he is shown with an erect phallus. Centuries later the Hindu god Shiva would be envisaged in just the same manner, as giver of life, lord of the animals, and deity over the unending cycles of creation and destruction.

Although the people of the Indus Valley probably observed most rites of faith in household shrines, one imposing structure

A resident of Mohenjo-daro douses himself with water drawn from a well within his home. The bathrooms of Harappan houses were tightly paved with fired bricks that were waterproofed with gypsum; the run-off exited through a chute at the base of the wall and flowed into a covered drain in the street. Such innovative plumbing, which included toilets in some dwellings, was more than a convenience: It helped reduce disease among the 40,000 or so Harappans who lived together at close quarters in the sweltering city.

in Mohenjo-daro may well have been a place of public worship. It was a large brick-lined bath, 8 feet deep, 23 feet wide and 39 feet long. Here, groups of citizens could have gathered to perform ritual washings — much as India's faithful still do in the Ganges River and in similar bathing tanks at some Hindu shrines. A flight of steps at either end descended into the bath; a surrounding cloister supported a wooden roof and housed a series of small chambers where bathers would have changed clothes or undergone personal rites. Adjacent to the main tank was a block of eight small private baths with second-floor rooms — possibly dwellings for priests. Cleanliness, both of body and spirit, seems to have been a Harappan passion.

After a Harappan citizen died, the body was laid to rest in a cemetery outside the walls of the city. The deceased was buried so that the head was to the north. Numerous pots containing food and water surrounded the body, and favorite pieces of jewelry were placed on the deceased for the journey to the world beyond the grave. Often the effects included toilet articles such as a copper mirror or a set of sticks for applying kohl, a mascara-like compound used for painting the eyes. Most people were placed directly into the earth, but at least one woman was bequeathed the distinction of a coffin made from cedar and rosewood.

The Harappan civilization endured 500 years without perceptible change. Its territory expanded, reaching east toward the Ganges and south into Gujarat, where new cities were founded. Trade with Mesopotamia languished for a time after the death of Sargon, then picked up again under the dynasty of the Sumerian king Ur-Nammu. Periodic high floods of the Indus took their toll, despite the best efforts of Harappan engineers. The valley's southern reaches were also subject to occasional earthquakes of great violence. One upheaval may have blocked the Indus with a massive ridge of extruded mud, creating a temporary lake; later, when the dam broke, the waters surged over Mohenjo-daro, inundating the city. But after each catastrophe, the citizens picked up their lives again. Some sections of Mohenjo-daro were rebuilt as many as eight times. In each reconstruction, the architects re-created the previous construction virtually brick for brick. Not a street line was shifted, not a house-front was extended beyond its former boundaries. Few civilizations have displayed such a degree of ingrained conservatism — or such remarkable staying power. Sometime during the nineteenth century BC, however, the Indus cities began to slip into permanent decline. No single cause seems to have been responsible. The region's climate may have changed, with the monsoon rains shifting to the east and leaving the valley too arid to sustain civilization. Many centuries of intensive cultivation coupled with disastrous changes in the course of the Indus River may at last have depleted the soils. And overly ambitious irrigation projects could have caused harmful salts to leach up from the water table, eventually poisoning the crops.

Flocks of sheep and goats, their numbers increasing to feed a growing population, may have denuded the hillsides, causing erosion and disrupting the natural watersheds. Just as damaging, Harappan loggers may have felled too many forests, both for timber and for firewood to bake the bricks used in building the cities. This disruption of the valley's ecology would have further reduced the amount of rainfall, thrusting a drought-prone area toward outright desert. At the same time, the Harappans' all-important

Harappan seals offer a vivid record of the animal species that flourished in the lush Indus Valley in the third millennium BC — including the zebu bull *(top)*, with its prominent hump; the so-called unicorn, apparently another type of bull with its head shown in profile; the Indian rhinoceros, distinguished by its platelike sections of skin; and the elephant, adorned here with a cloth. Although many seals found in the region bear similar designs, the inscriptions are bewilderingly diverse, suggesting that they represent proper names: Harappan merchants used the seals as a kind of trademark, impressing them on clay tags to label their goods.

trade seemed to wither. Scribes in Mesopotamia recorded rich shipments from the Indus Valley until around 1800 BC, when they suddenly ceased. Moreover, the small, settled populations of Central Asia began to mobilize and expand. Tribes of riders from the Iranian plateau began infiltrating the Baluchistan hills and may have merged with village cultures.

Whatever the reason, the Harappans largely abandoned their Indus Valley cities toward the end of the eighteenth century BC. Some of the citizens moved east into Rajasthan and the Ganges watershed. Others headed south to Gujarat, where the seaport at Lothal continued to flourish for a time. Then Lothal, too, was abandoned, and its inhabitants merged with the Stone Age tribes of the Deccan Plateau in central India and others in southern India.

Squatters arrived from the countryside and took over the vacated citadels and housing blocks at Mohenjo-daro and at Harappa. Flimsy partitions of inferior brick now divided the courtyards, and a shambles of slumlike dwellings engulfed the granaries that had belonged to the state. Crude new types of pottery and metalwork replaced the more refined objects of Harappan workshops.

But Harappan influence did not entirely disappear. Village life continued, and crafts and technical skills survived. The urban heritage was passed on to the east, where it engendered the emergence of cities in the Ganges valley and North India. Certain ideas and beliefs — the reverence for animals, a tendency toward mysticism as expressed by the Shiva-like deity of the seals — had laid permanent claim on the consciousness of the people of India, and these somber notes of Harappan ideology would continue to reverberate through the coming centuries.

Even before the Indus Valley builders laid their first course of brick, an offshoot of civilized endeavor was unfolding in the tropical forests and moist alluvial plains of Southeast Asia. The people involved practiced a simple economy, never reaching beyond the stage of village agriculture and craftsmanship. But within these limits their accomplishments were remarkable.

The landscape of Southeast Asia is complex and convoluted. Steep mountain ridges drop abruptly to deep river valleys. Dense forests of bamboo, teak, and giant fern cloak the hillsides; they give way, at lower elevations, to savannah plateaus and then to sparsely wooded swampland. The coastline, deeply indented, bends and twists along thousands of miles of mangrove swamp and sandy, palm-fringed beach. To the south, across the China Sea, rise the summits of Malaysia and the far-flung archipelagoes of Indonesia and the Philippines.

The climate, by contrast, is highly predictable. Torrential rains drench the region seasonally, swept in from the Indian Ocean by the hot, heavy air masses of the southwest monsoon. A cool, dry period always follows.

Sometime before the fifth millennium BC, several jungle tribes of hunters and gatherers established small village communities throughout the area. A number took up residence along the coast, where they fished, collected crabs and coconuts, fired pottery, and crafted tools of stone. Others moved into limestone caves in the forested uplands. An abundance of wildlife and a profusion of edible plants supplied a steady and varied diet. Dwellers in the so-called Spirit Cave, in what would later be northwest Thailand, evidently dined on beans, water chestnuts, melons, and nuts. They also chewed betel nut, which blackened their teeth but treated their palates to a tangy, astringent savor.

The Kiln's Outpouring

The working of clay ranks among the oldest of human crafts. The first clay figurines and vessels were simply left in the sun to harden, but by 7000 BC, potters in the Near East were firing their wares in kilns — a step that was soon adopted elsewhere because it yielded much sturdier objects. By the dawn of civilization, artisans using simple tools were creating ceramics as elegant as they were serviceable. Potters of the Ban Chiang culture in Thailand made fine jars like the ones below by tempering their clay with rice husks, forming it into hollow cylinders, and then paddling the cylinders into shape around anvils that lent form to the pots before they were fired.

Such handcrafting — slow and arduous — remained the rule in Thailand. But elsewhere, the potter's wheel speeded the process. By 3000 BC, hand-turned wheels in Sumer and Egypt were fostering workshops whose goods were exported far and wide. By 1600, potters from Crete to China were using wheels powered by pedals. The centrifugal force from the wheel was deftly exploited by the artisan, whose graceful creations were then embellished with bright glazes or intricate brushwork. No aspect of civilized life was left untouched by these advances: Decorative and durable ceramics, such as those pictured here and on the following pages, were turned out in great quantity to stock kitchens and dining halls, storage rooms and sanctuaries.

Chinese vase painted in geometric pattern

Jars from Ban Chiang culture

As early as 7000 BC, the people of Southeast Asia had begun planting and harvesting their own crops. The beans stored in the Spirit Cave were domestic varieties. So was the rice. The grain grew wild along marshy riverbanks throughout Southeast Asia, from the delta lands of what would become Burma to as far east as the Yangtze River in China. Using serrated stone knives, tribespeople cut the stalks of the wild grain and threshed out the few kernels each stalk provided. As time went on, they learned to increase their yields by cultivating the plant in prepared paddies. It was laborious, backbreaking work, for each seedling had to be transplanted, roots and all, and then it had to be kept under shallow water while the plant matured. But the region's monsoon climate, with its copious and dependable rainfall, offered an ideal setting for the growing of this crop.

Some of the region's rice farmers lived in the rolling, lightly forested grasslands of the Khorat Plateau on what is now northeast Thailand. They had moved up from the low country around 3600 BC, carrying their seeds with them and leading small trains of domesticated animals. These would have included dogs, pigs, and a variety of cattle closely related to the zebu of India. Their villages were clusters of thatched bamboo huts raised on stilts to keep them above the rainy-season muds. To clear the land for planting in dry fields, they used a slash-and-burn technique, chopping down trees and brush, burning the wood, and then working the soil with hand-held digging sticks. The damper areas, set aside for rice cultivation, were plotted into paddies with surrounding mud dikes to hold in the water. Life was simple and hard.

Yet the Khorat settlers practiced highly sophisticated manufacturing skills quite unexpected in an isolated land of small villages. How they happened on their ideas is not known; the methods may have been learned through some unexplained contact with other villages to the west, or they may simply have sprung from a sort of internal genius. Whatever the case, these rice farmers were strikingly adept at both ceramics and metallurgy.

Hedgehog vase from Cyclades Islands

Lid to Harappan jar

Village potters at Ban Chiang, a 120-acre settlement not far from the Mekong River valley on the plateau's northern edge, developed a range of ceramics as elegant in profile and inventive in design as any that were being produced in the urban centers of Mesopotamia or India. Other villages nearby, such as Non Nok Tha to the south, produced artifacts of similar quality. Just as ingenious were the metalworkers of Khorat. By the year 2000 BC, and perhaps as much earlier as 500 years before that, they had become experts at casting tools and ornaments of bronze — in much the same manner as artisans in Mesopotamia, more than 3,000 miles to the west.

The method of producing bronze — an alloy that combines copper with one of several other metals — requires great technical proficiency. The key element in the process is copper, which can be extracted from its ore with relative ease, compared with most base metals. Pure copper by itself, in fact, can be molded or hammered into useful shapes, but the metal has a severe drawback: During the smelting process, it has a tendency to oxidize. The small bubbles of gas that collect are trapped, and they make the metal brittle and weak.

Bronze, on the other hand, does not oxidize and therefore is much more durable than copper and more suitable for fashioning into tools and weapons. Bronze can be produced by adding a small percentage of lead, antimony, or arsenic to the copper; in Mesopotamia, the first smiths used arsenic, which was often present in the copper ore itself. But the best additive by far is tin, and here the Khorat smiths enjoyed a decided advantage. Southeast Asia is the world's richest source of tin, and one of the few places where copper and tin occur naturally in close proximity. The Southeast Asians probably panned tin ore from their rivers, much as a prospector would pan for gold. They mined the copper from mountainsides north and west of the Khorat Plateau. In lowland villages they smelted the metals in clay-lined pits or crucibles.

Egyptian vase appliquéd with diorite

Minoan mixing bowl with ceramic flowers

They reinforced the clay with rice husks to keep it intact at high temperatures. And they brought their fires to the intensity necessary to melt copper — roughly 1,983° F. — by means of hollow bamboo tubes through which they blew a steady stream of air over the coals; later, they developed a simple bellows to fan the coals. The molten bronze was poured off into sandstone molds made in the shape of the desired object. The casting was allowed to cool, and then the mold was opened. Using this method, an artisan at Non Nok Tha cast a bronze blade for a digging stick, giving it a socket for attaching a handle. It was one of the world's oldest known socketed tools.

Virtually all the metal objects at Ban Chiang — ax heads, spear tips, and bracelets — were cast from bronze. And the metal produced by the Khorat smiths was of the highest quality. For durability and hardness, the optimum proportion of tin to copper is 10 percent. Most of the Khorat bronzes fall into this category, which places their creators in the metalworking vanguard of their day.

Surprisingly — considering their technological skills — the Khorat people built no cities, erected no temples, appointed no rulers. They generated none of the elaborate political trappings or rigid social stratification that elsewhere marked civilized life. Instead of developing a system of writing, they seem to have been dependent on the spoken word to conduct their business and on oral tradition to recount the history of their civilization. The villagers lived simply, planting their rice and turning out their pottery and bronzes — and would continue to do so without significant change or interruption for the next 1,000 years.

Yet the early Southeast Asian culture was not stagnant. Some type of barter must have existed between villages. Ban Chiang, for example, appears to have been a regional center for production that supplied essentials to the surrounding countryside. There must also have been periods of travel or migration to other areas, for gradually the techniques of rice planting began to percolate throughout Southeast Asia and beyond. People speaking one of the region's original languages, Austro-Thai, moved

Boot-shaped vessel from Anatolia

Minoan basket-shaped vase with double axes

across the Pacific Ocean, to New Zealand, Easter Island, Hawaii, and points between.

Their influence also spread northeast, farther into China. The word for *copper* in ancient Chinese was *tong*. There is reason to believe that the Chinese borrowed the term directly from Austro-Thai. It is likely that the Chinese adopted from the Khorat people the basic techniques of metalworking as well, perhaps sometime in the second millennium BC, early in the emergence of the civilization that would become the world's most enduring.

Clusters of primitive farmers had already put down roots throughout much of China by the dawn of the third millennium. In the marshes at the mouth of the Yangtze River in South China, for example, villagers lived in solidly constructed timber houses raised on wooden pilings — much like those in Southeast Asia. They made tools of bone and wood, wove cloth, carved ornaments of ivory, and fashioned a coarse black pottery. Earlier, as hunters, they had stalked the most challenging game — elephants, rhinoceroses, bears, and tigers. They also hunted wild sheep, deer, monkeys, and turtles. Having long since tamed both dogs and pigs, the villagers would soon harness the water buffalo for transport and plowing. Their staple crop was rice, which they may have learned to cultivate from earlier contact with the Southeast Asians.

A different type of agriculture flourished in the steppelike uplands of northern China. Along the middle reaches of the Yellow River, China's mightiest watercourse, a vast plateau lay blanketed under a thick layer of compacted yellow dust called loess. The loess was carried by the northwest wind, which over the millennia picked up surface soil from the Gobi Desert 600 miles away and deposited it along the Yellow River in depths up to 450 feet. The wind, and occasional flash floods, continually reshaped the land, carving the loess into fantastic panoramas of a monochromatic golden hue — dunes, gullies, cliffs, terraces, and towers. A perpetual tawny haze tinted the air. Rainfall was less than twenty inches a year — though fortunately for farmers it fell mostly in summer. Temperatures in July and August could be blistering. Winters were an arid desolation of fierce wind and biting cold.

Yet for China's early agriculturalists, the loess plateau had some advantages. No forests needed clearing; no thick, heavy sod required cutting before planting could begin. The settlers merely had to burn off the light grass cover and turn the powdery soil with simple digging sticks. Further, the loess had an exceptionally high mineral content, and it proved inexhaustably fertile.

Despite the contradictory conditions, this region would provide northern China's first important agricultural surpluses and so give rise to the culture that would eventually hold sway over most of eastern Asia. By the third millennium peasants were living in compact villages dug into loess terraces overlooking the Yellow River and its tributaries. The climate was too severe for rice; instead, the main crop was millet, a grain that had originally grown wild in the region.

One important settlement took shape at Banpo in Shaanxi Province, on the Wei River, one of the Yellow's main branches. The village covered about twelve acres on a terrace overlooking the river. The houses were bunched together in a central compound, which the villagers surrounded with a large ditch — for drainage, defense, or both. Each dwelling consisted of a single room, either round, square, or rectangular in shape and usually measuring between ten and seventeen feet in diameter or length. Many of the houses were built a few feet into the ground so that the floor was recessed below the outside level. Wooden posts supported upper walls of wattle and daub. The roofs, which were constructed of twigs and reeds and plastered in mud, jutted out over the walls of the houses to provide extra protection from the rain. A ramplike entrance permitted access to each house. Between the houses, the villagers dug pits where they stored many of their possessions, especially grain. There were also a number of pens for keeping livestock.

Over time, the settlement grew into a thriving community of perhaps 600 people. To accommodate everyone inside the boundary of the village ditch, the citizens erected in the central plaza a large communal house, which they partitioned into rooms for individual families, each with its own hearth.

The villagers lived on a variety of foods. In addition to millet, they raised and gathered native vegetables, fruits, and nuts; among these were cabbages, blackberries, chestnuts, hazelnuts, and pine nuts. For meat, they commonly kept pigs and dogs; and in rare cases they also raised cattle, sheep, or goats.

To make cloth, they harvested hemp and spun its fibers into thread, which they then wove together. There is also evidence that the villagers made silk: Clay replicas of silkworms found in the area suggest that they raised the worms, or caterpillars, which spun the cocoons that provided the shimmering fibers of silk.

Banpo artisans fashioned the tools and ornaments that were used by Neolithic farmers everywhere — stone knives, axes, sickles, tips for digging sticks, and pottery of various sorts. Even at this early stage, they exhibited a rare degree of skill and imagination. The village pottery works, at the eastern edge of the dwelling area, comprised no fewer than six kilns. Here, the Banpo potters fired their earthenware vessels into an extraordinary variety of shapes, sizes, designs, and finishes, ranging from simple gray bowls and urns for everyday use to elegant ritual pieces adorned with abstract patterns of whorls and triangles, or lifelike depictions of birds, fish, frogs, and human faces.

Many hundreds of similar communities sprang up in the loess country and in adjoining regions to the south and east; from the name of one of the villages, these people later came to be known collectively as the Yangshao culture. For all their similarities, these communities nevertheless enjoyed a certain amount of individualization. Styles of pottery, and perhaps local customs, varied considerably from place to place. Farther east, on the Shandong Peninsula, which juts into the Yellow Sea near the mouth of the Yellow River, the Dawenkou people made handsome ceramic pitchers in the form of pigs and other animals and fashioned exquisite ornaments of jade, ivory, and bone with turquoise inlay. Yet a common framework sustained them all: an agriculture based on millet and swine and a settled way of life on upland terraces overlooking the valley of the Yellow River and its tributary streams.

Around the middle of the third millennium, the traditions among these people began to change. The transformations began first along the lower course of the Yellow River and extended outward beyond the Yangshao territory and other regions to the north and east. A burgeoning agricultural economy began to create the trappings of civilization. Villages grew larger, more prosperous, and more socially organized. Groups of people began to make contact with each other over greater distances, perhaps to trade. The people, called Longshan in this stage of their evolution, began to progress materially. Differences between rich and poor increased sharply. In the community livestock pens, other animals now joined the pigs; goats, sheep, cattle, and chickens brought a pleasant variety to the diet of pork and millet.

Longshan pottery took on a new and somewhat austere elegance. While the Yangshao potters had handcrafted their wares from coils of clay, the Longshan artisans

147

employed the potter's wheel. They redesigned their kilns to achieve greater control over the firing process and to produce higher temperatures; as a result, they could turn out elegant vessels with walls not much thicker than eggshells.

Along with these technological advances, the Longshan people seem to have adopted a more defensive posture than their predecessors. Besides the usual farm implements of flaked and polished stone, their artisans produced larger numbers of spear points and arrowheads. Around each settlement, the Longshan erected a massive barricade of stamped earth, which was probably intended as a line of defense against attack. Armed conflict seems to have been an integral part of their culture.

While the Yangshao villagers buried their dead in graveyards several miles outside their residential areas, their successors interred bodies within the town ramparts. Often the Longshan graves were dug beneath the floor of the houses; deceased children, placed in funeral urns, were cemented into the walls of the foundation. The Longshan methods of burial suggest that another custom followed by these people was ancestor worship. Each family kept its forebears close at hand, their bodies covered over but their spirits ever present.

Wider changes took place among the people. Clan leaders emerged, men successful in battle and dominant in village affairs. Degrees of influence and wealth began to separate the Longshan people into social classes, with an aristocracy holding sway over the rest. Some men fought and plundered; others raised the animals and harvested the millet.

The leaders of the aristocracy naturally surrounded themselves with assistants and advisers, including shamans, whose main function was to foretell the future. These holy men read the stars in order to predict the coming of the seasons and thus the best times for planting and harvesting. And they developed other methods of divination for various occasions. One technique entailed roasting animal bones — specifically the shoulder blades of sheep, pigs, or cattle; from the cracks that the heat produced, the priests would attempt to divine the outcome of hunting excursions and military campaigns, to foretell births and deaths, and to interpret dreams and other omens.

While the Longshan leaders seem to have made frequent war, their greatest battle was against the forces of nature. The Yellow River is the world's most hazardous watercourse. Its cargo of suspended loess builds up in the riverbed, causing the Yellow to overflow its banks periodically and roll out across the floodplain, submerging thousands of square miles. More threatening to those who lived near it, the Yellow has radically changed course at least twenty-six times in recorded history. The Chinese call it their River of Sorrow. It has taken lives beyond counting.

Because of the danger, the early inhabitants avoided settling in the great central plain, a potentially fertile region formed of silt carried down from the loess country by the river. But the urge to cultivate the plain was always strong. And the first successful attempts that were made to settle there seem to have occurred during the Longshan period, when great levees, drainage canals, and impoundments were raised along stretches of the Yellow River.

Chinese legend gives credit for this taming of the Yellow River to one of the civilization's early emperors, Yu the Great, who was said to have lived in the twenty-third century BC. Like cultural heroes the world over, Yu was a man possessing mythic power; he descended from a line of supernatural ancestors. Yu's earliest forebear sprang into the world with a dragon's body. This miraculous creature was the first of China's legendary Three Sovereigns, and he is honored for having invented the art of

This palatial compound at the town of Erlitou, its entryway guarded by a stout barricade, was a hive of political activity in the late days of China's Xia dynasty: It may well have housed the rulers of that line, who made their capital here beginning around the year 2000 BC. Erected on a solid platform of compressed earth, the compound featured a spacious courtyard for ceremonial functions and a main hall where dignitaries convened; both the hall and the smaller chambers ringing the courtyard were shielded from the elements by thick wattle-and-daub walls and a thatched roof. Beyond the walls lay clusters of houses, kilns, and storage pits where hundreds labored in support of the compound.

divination and for having devised the nets that were used in hunting and fishing.

Yu himself achieved his eminence in 2205 BC, the legends relate, as a reward for ending the flood that annually had ravaged China's central plain for thirteen calamitous years. Marshaling all the people of north China, he built a vast system of dikes and drainage channels that confined the river to its own channel. "We should have been fish," a later Chinese saying goes, "but for Yu."

Yu the Great may have been a figure of legend. But someone like him, some powerful and farsighted leader or group of leaders, is likely to have emerged during the Longshan period. The struggle against the Yellow River, the first notable attempts at wide-scale flood control, the beginnings of settlement in the rich central plain, all suggest the presence of an increasingly well-organized social authority. Indeed, the ancient scrolls relate as much. For there it is written that Yu the Great was the founding patriarch of China's first historically recorded dynasty, the Xia.

Few particulars are known about the Xia; the earliest listing of their succession of emperors appears in classical texts written nearly 2,000 years after the fact. Apparently the Xia's imperial capital, at Erlitou in southern Shaanxi, belonged to the final stages of Longshan culture and shared most of its perils and advantages.

Like the Longshan, the Xia dynasty moved China several steps into the future. Their emperors assembled armies and commandeered large work forces to build city walls and palaces with foundations of stamped earth. Xia artisans carved jade into handsome tools and ornaments. Xia bronze weapons gave warriors a victorious technology, and their cast-bronze vessels added elegance to royal ceremonies. Imperial scholars may already have been using archetypal pictograms, derived from earlier clan symbols, that would evolve into the national script. Later cultures credit the Xia with creating China's original calendar.

The dynasty's advances came about under a harsh rule. The Xia emperors seem to have imposed their will through a combination of armed might and ceremonial terror, based in part on a cult of human sacrifice. At the capital of Erlitou, the remains of victims were later discovered with their hands tied and heads missing.

The full extent of Xia power, and the influence it wielded across the 1,000-mile sweep of northern China, is not entirely clear. The Xia undoubtedly traded with other peoples on the periphery of their empire. There surely were connections with the rice-growing inhabitants in southern China. But to the rulers of Xia, these outlanders were not much more than uncivilized barbarians. The center of the universe, ordained by heaven, was the throne of the Xia emperor.

Sixteen emperors in succession followed Yu the Great, according to the legend, for a total span of 439 years. Then the dynasty fell victim to another and stronger indigenous people, the Shang, who came to power midway through the eighteenth century BC. The Shang adopted the Xia heritage and launched the Chinese people toward cultural prominence in Asia — a feat accomplished even as the rest of the civilized world was being shaken to its foundation. In Mesopotamia, the Babylonians — heirs to the rich Sumerian legacy of literacy and law-giving — fell subject to tribespeople sweeping down from the northeast. On Crete, the exuberant Minoan culture was being extinguished, although some of its brilliance would later be reflected in the commercial and artistic genius of the Greek city-states. Along the Nile, the proud spirit of the pharaohs would survive only a few centuries before internal strife and alien armies depleted the realm. Of the first great civilizations, only China would emerge from the tumult with its sovereignty unquestioned and its traditions intact.

THE FRUITS OF EXCHANGE

Although their fields produced an abundance of grain, the people of the first civilizations lacked many other essential resources. To obtain the raw materials needed for making weapons, tools, and luxury items for the wealthy, ancient city dwellers relied on traders who linked them to distant mines and quarries. Driven by the demands of kings, or lured by the glitter of profit, adventurous merchants led trains of donkeys through mountains or deserts and piloted small ships across treacherous waters. A successful trader might return to his home city with logs to buttress the walls of a palace or gold and silver to be transformed on a jeweler's workbench.

Sumer, whose plains yielded no worthwhile raw materials, depended entirely on trade. The stone chiseled by sculptors, the copper and tin smelted by bronzesmiths, even the timber used by Sumer's carpenters had to be imported. In exchange for such vital commodities, the cities of Mesopotamia bartered surplus grain and the finished work of their peerless artisans. With immense profits at stake, freewheeling merchants in Sumerian ports struck deals of great complexity.

Egypt, in contrast, boasted few independent merchants. The pharaoh controlled the wealth of the country, and for him trade was a matter of diplomacy. Typically, a trade deal was arranged by the pharaoh's ambassadors as an exchange of gifts with a foreign monarch. Most often, the pharaoh paid for his purchases with gold, which poured in from Egypt's fabulous mines. The Egyptian military also took an active hand in trade. Heavily armed expeditions pushed far down the Red Sea coast or plunged deep into the African interior, returning with ebony, ivory, incense, panther skins, and ostrich feathers.

In order to obtain certain kinds of commodities, the pharaoh's ministers relied at times on foreign merchants. Often these visitors were Minoans, the seafaring traders who profited mightily as brokers shuttling between Mediterranean ports with products to sell.

Like the Minoans, the people of Dilmun, a largely desolate Persian Gulf island now known as Bahrein, served as go-betweens for international trade. Dilmun's only native products of value were the tasty onions for which it was famous, but the island offered a convenient point of exchange for goods from Sumer and the rich Indus Valley far to the east. Its bustling markets handled cotton, metals, and gems from the Indus, as well as copper from Oman and wood from

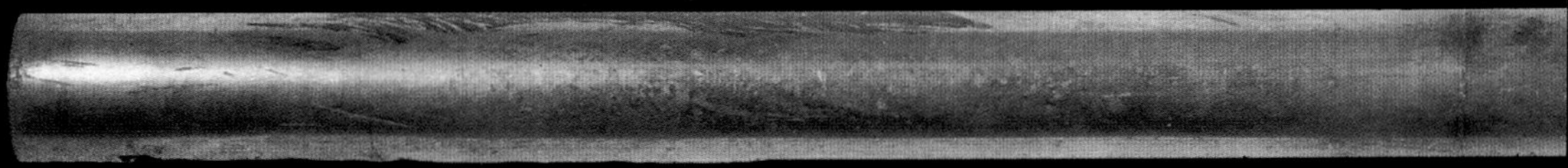

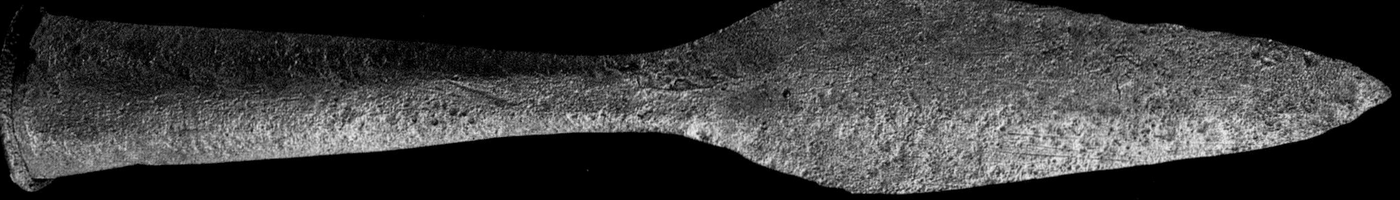

Cretan spearhead

Egyptian ax

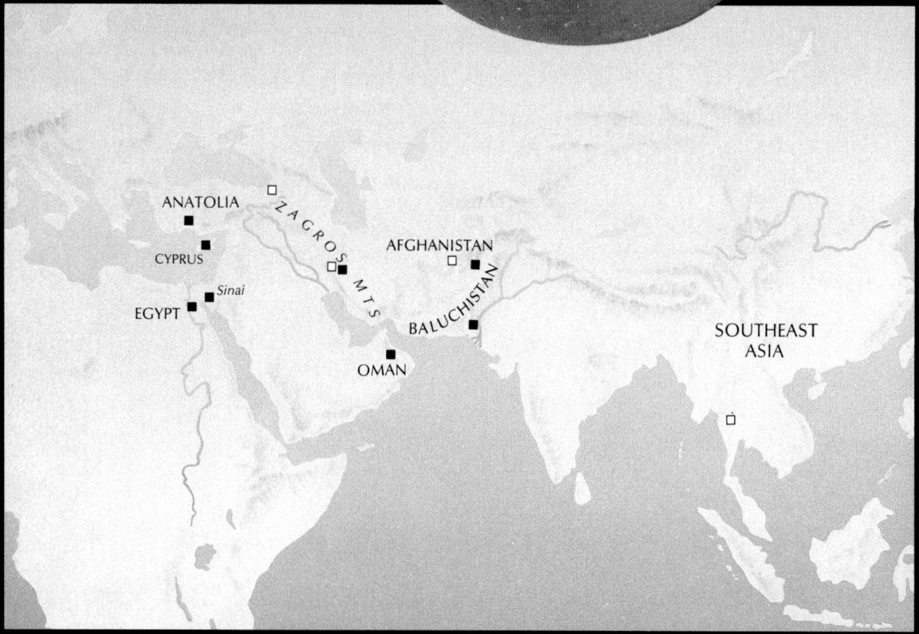

Major sources of copper *(black)* and tin *(white)*

Egyptian battle ax with silver handle

Egyptian knife with wooden handle

THE QUEST FOR BRONZE

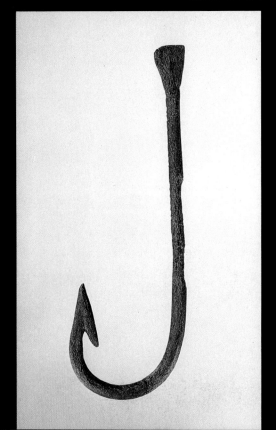

Among the most valued commodities marketed on the island of Dilmun or traded by Crete's merchant seamen was the greenish ore known as malachite. Smelting the ore in charcoal furnaces reduced it to copper, the first widely used metal. A strong yet malleable material, copper could be hammered or cast into a variety of art objects and utensils. Copper axheads, swords, knives, and spearpoints gave soldiers an advantage over enemies with weapons of brittle stone.

After about 3000 BC, the harder and more durable bronze — an alloy that generally combined copper and tin — began to replace copper as the metal of choice for weapons and armor. But tin was scarce at first, and the production of bronze was limited. The search for tin ore stretched trade networks far to the east and west, even beyond the edges of the world known to the early civilized peoples. The Minoans made bronze with tin from the Mediterranean or, possibly, England. The Sumerians obtained tin from sources in the Zagros Mountains and Afghanistan, while the Egyptians may have imported it from Anatolia.

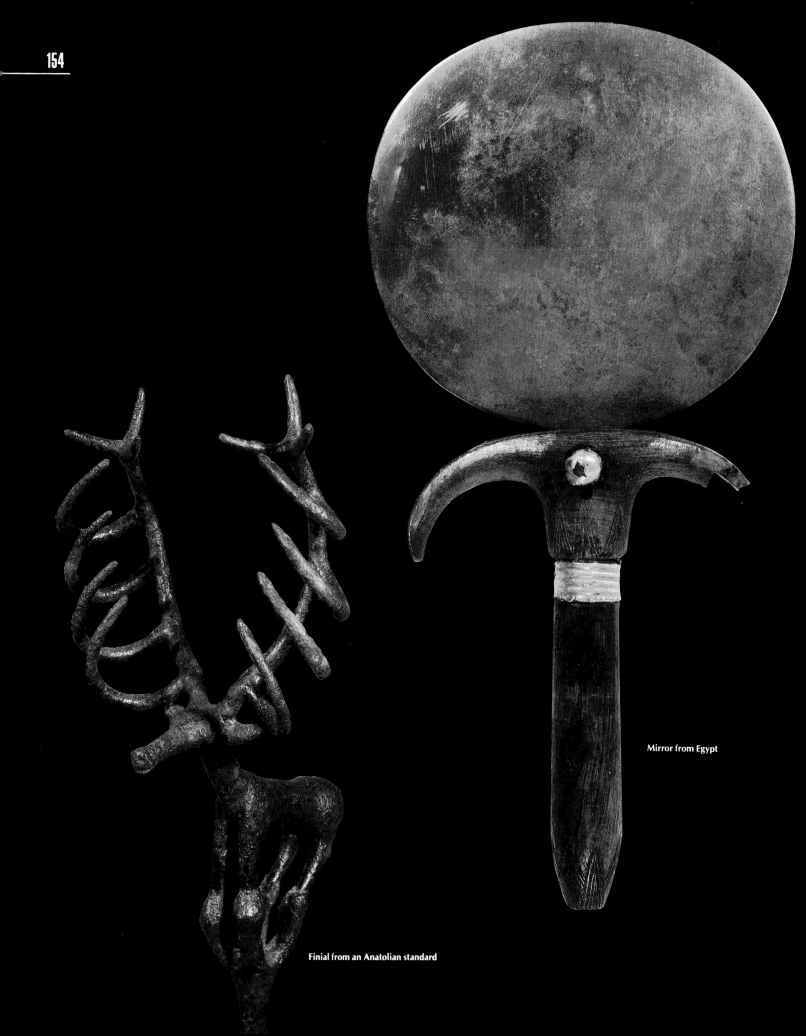

Finial from an Anatolian standard

Mirror from Egypt

Minoan skillet

Copper altar and sacred vessels from Egypt

Egyptian copper razor

Silver ax from Afghanistan

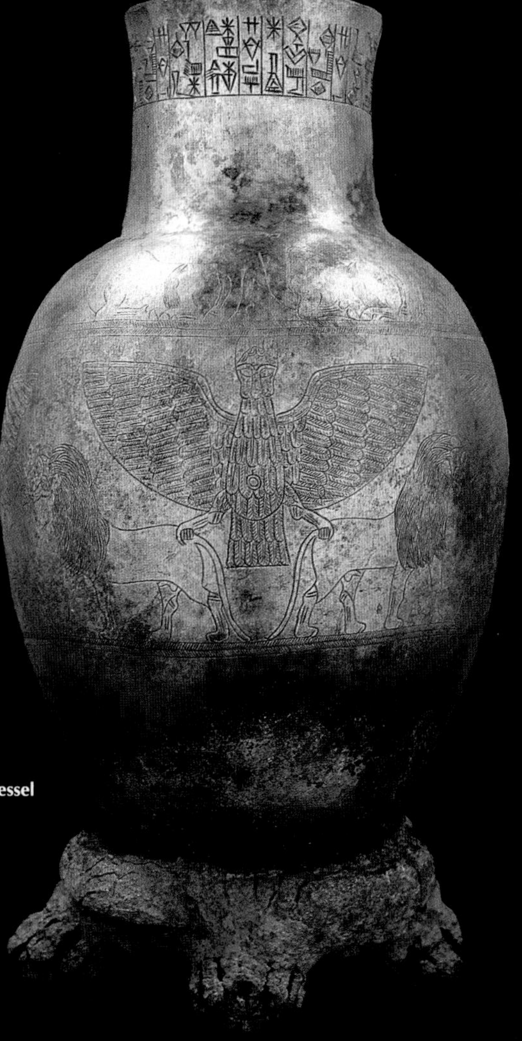

Sumerian ceremonial vessel

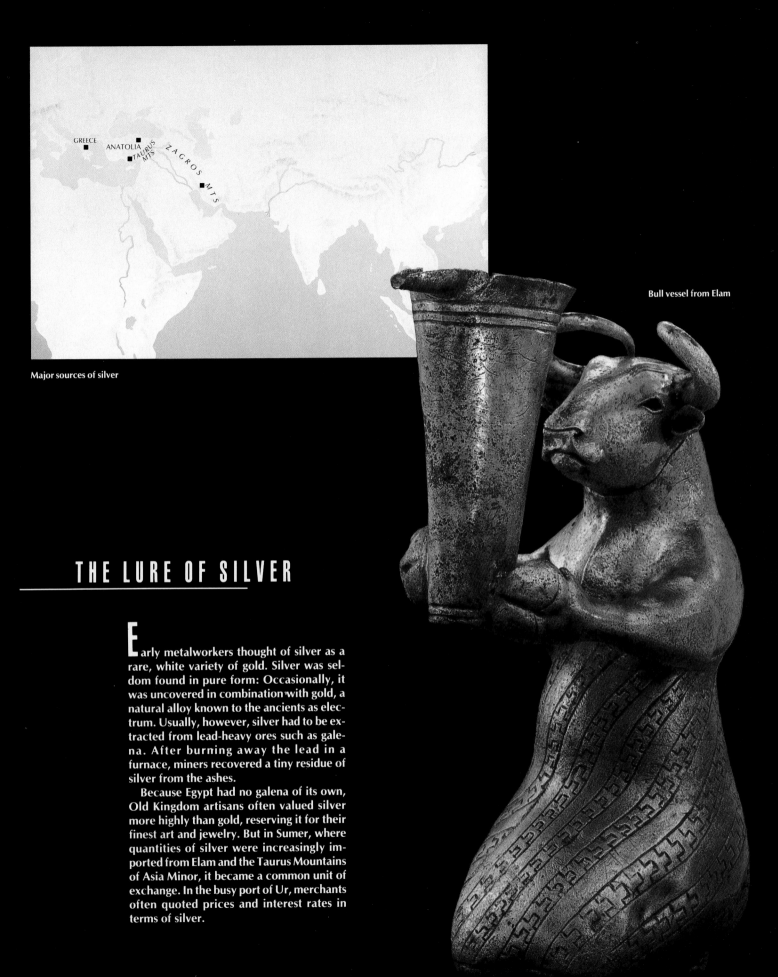

Major sources of silver

Bull vessel from Elam

THE LURE OF SILVER

Early metalworkers thought of silver as a rare, white variety of gold. Silver was seldom found in pure form: Occasionally, it was uncovered in combination with gold, a natural alloy known to the ancients as electrum. Usually, however, silver had to be extracted from lead-heavy ores such as galena. After burning away the lead in a furnace, miners recovered a tiny residue of silver from the ashes.

Because Egypt had no galena of its own, Old Kingdom artisans often valued silver more highly than gold, reserving it for their finest art and jewelry. But in Sumer, where quantities of silver were increasingly imported from Elam and the Taurus Mountains of Asia Minor, it became a common unit of exchange. In the busy port of Ur, merchants often quoted prices and interest rates in terms of silver.

The people of the first civilizations cherished gold for its beauty, rarity, and durability. Because the yellow metal would not corrode or even tarnish, it seemed eternal: Artisans treated gold with reverence, priests used it for sacred ornamentation in their temples, and kings were buried with gold that was meant to accompany them to the afterlife.

The first gold collected by civilized people was likely in nugget form, panned from the gravel of streambeds or from the sands of long-dead rivers. But alluvial stocks in many areas quickly played out, forcing local rulers to slake their thirst for gold through trade. Some gold could be found in Arabia, but usually rulers looked to Egypt, where enormous

A LUST FOR GOLD

quantities of the precious mineral lay in deserts east of the Nile and in Nubian mines under Egyptian control. So rich were these deposits that foreigners believed gold in Egypt to be "as common as dust."

Major sources of gold

Dagger from a royal burial at Ur

Sumerian helmet

Ewer from Anatolia

Egyptian head of Horus

Sumerian cup

Human-headed bison from Syria

Minoan pendant

Minoan bull's-head earring

Necklace from Greece

Egyptian necklace of golden flies

Pendant from the Indus Valley

Sumerian necklace

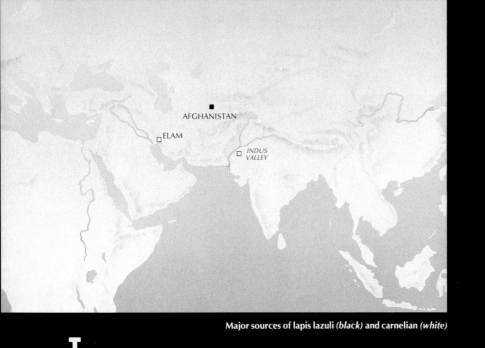

Major sources of lapis lazuli *(black)* and carnelian *(white)*

AFGHANISTAN

ELAM

INDUS
VALLEY

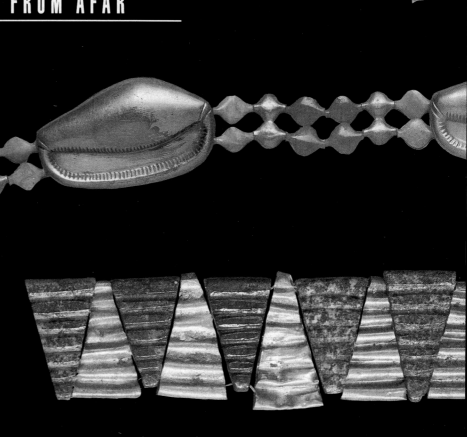

Sumerian gold-leaf necklace
with lapis and carnelian

GEMSTONES FROM AFAR

The expansion of trade greatly increased the variety of materials available to jewelers. Wealthy members of society could adorn themselves not only with gold and silver but with rare gems and colorful stones brought from remote mines. One stone that announced the high status of its wearer was lapis lazuli, a blue mineral often shot through with flecks of sparkling yellow pyrite. Most of the lapis used by ancient jewelers came from the region of Badakhshan, in Afghanistan. As early as 2500 BC, caravans delivered Afghan lapis to merchants in the Indus Valley, who shipped it to Sumer and Egypt.

Another popular stone was the translucent carnelian, mined chiefly in Elam and in the mountains of the Indus region. Traders bore numerous high-quality, bright-red carnelians from the Indus Valley to the Sumerian port of Ur, probably by way of Dilmun.

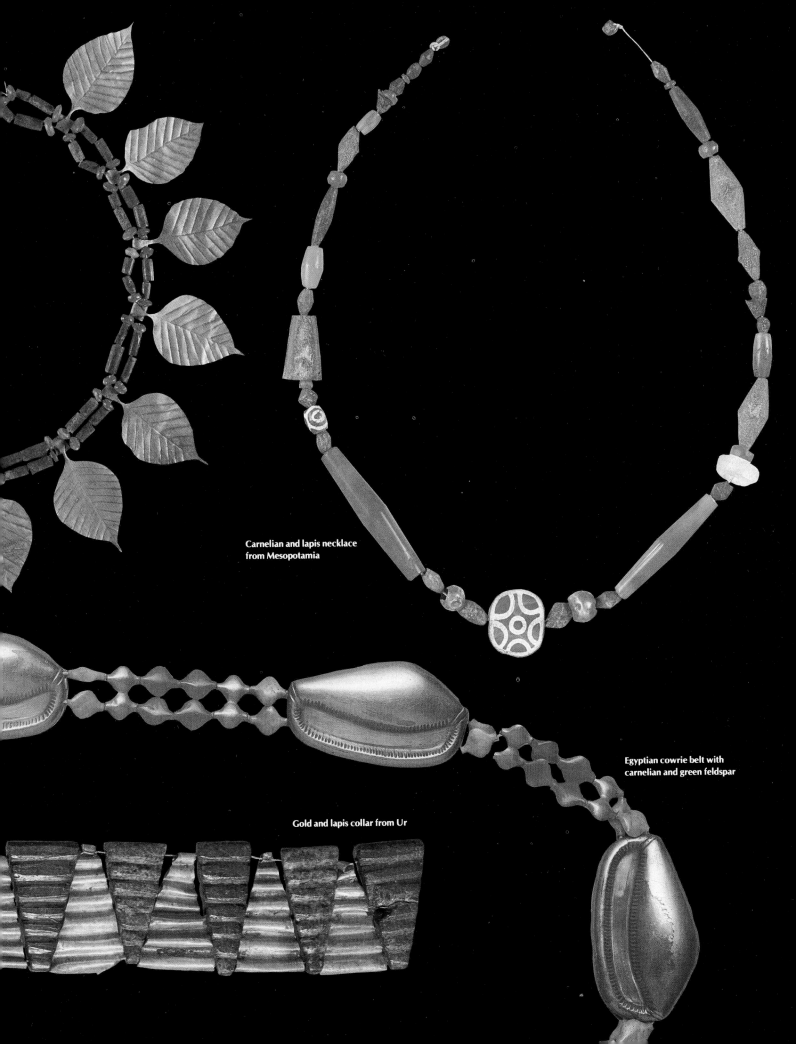

Carnelian and lapis necklace
from Mesopotamia

Egyptian cowrie belt with
carnelian and green feldspar

Gold and lapis collar from Ur

3000 BC	2900 BC	2800 BC	2700 BC	2600 BC	2500 BC	2400 BC	2300 BC

MESOPOTAMIA

3000 BC: Sumerian city-states flourish. Lagash and Uruk become the most powerful city-states.

Sumerians trade with the peoples of Asia Minor, Syria, Elam, and the island of Dilmun (Bahrein) in the Persian Gulf.

2700 BC: Celebrated king Gilgamesh rules over the city of Uruk.

2500 BC: First dynasty of Ur begins. Members of the royal family are buried there with great pomp.

2400 BC: Lugalzaggesi of Umma conquers Lagash and unifies Sumer.

Sargon I of Akkad defeats Lugalzaggesi and unites his land with Sumer. He conquers Elam, Syria, and southeastern Asia Minor.

2300 BC: Naram-Sin, grandson of Sargon I, claims divinity and calls himself "King of the Four Quarters," meaning the world.

Gutians invade the region and exert their influence for half a century.

EGYPT

3000 BC: First pharaohs rule at Memphis following the unification of Upper Egypt (the Nile Valley) and Lower Egypt (the Delta).

Cities arise at Abydos, Elephantine, and Hierakonpolis.

2700 BC: Djoser becomes king. His architect, Imhotep, designs the Step Pyramid at Saqqara.

2600 BC: Kings dispatch quarrying and mining expeditions to Nubia.

Sun cult develops at Heliopolis.

Khufu (Cheops) builds the Great Pyramid at Giza.

MEDITERRANEAN

2800 BC: Troy and other coastal cities are settled along the western fringe of Asia Minor.

Towns develop in Syria and Palestine, and later they are fortified.

People on the island of Malta build megalithic temples.

2700 BC: The Minoans on Crete begin active trade in the Mediterranean, traveling as far as Egypt.

2500 BC: Megalithic building spreads from Malta through the western Mediterranean to the Atlantic, extending eventually from Morocco to Sweden.

ASIA

2500 BC: Harappan civilization rises and flourishes in the Indus Valley.

2300 BC: Trade between Harappans and Sumerians reaches its height.

People of Southeast Asia and southern China fashion bronze tools using advanced metalworking techniques.

Time Frame: 3000-1500 BC

2200 BC	2100 BC	2000 BC	1900 BC	1800 BC	1700 BC	1600 BC	1500 BC
	Ur-Nammu of Ur reunites the region under Sumerian leadership. He builds the famous ziggurat and records the first collection of laws.	Elamites from the Zagros Mountains and Amorites from upper Mesopotamia invade Sumer and destroy the city of Ur. The Akkadian language supplants the Sumerian tongue. Babylonian mathematics reaches a high level with a sexagesimal system.		Hammurabi of Babylon — author of the great code of law — comes to power. His empire stretches from the Persian Gulf to Syria.			The Hammurabi dynasty ends. Hittites destroy Babylon.
Pharaohs lose power as regional leaders grow in strength.	Mentuhotpe II establishes central authority at Thebes and represses local rulers.		Ammenemes III pursues irrigation projects and establishes copper mines in the Sinai peninsula.		The Hyksos invade Lower Egypt.		
		Minoans build great palaces on Crete and establish colonies on other Mediterranean islands and in Asia Minor. Cities on the island of Cyprus exploit copper resources to trade with the peoples of the Levant.			Minoans develop the script known as Linear A.	Palace at Knossos on Crete is destroyed, only to be rebuilt. Minoan colonies flourish on Thera and other islands.	Volcano erupts on Thera and destroys the island. Knossos is leveled again, and Minoan civilization disintegrates.
Xia dynasty begins in China with Emperor Yu the Great.		Cities of Mohenjo-daro and Harappa prosper in the Indus Valley.	Indus Valley civilization begins to disintegrate.		Shang dynasty supplants Xia dynasty in China.		

BIBLIOGRAPHY

BOOKS

Adams, Robert McC.:
Heartland of Cities: Surveys of Ancient Settlement and Land Use on the Central Floodplain of the Euphrates. Chicago: University of Chicago Press, 1981.
Land behind Baghdad: A History of Settlement on the Diyala Plains. Chicago: University of Chicago Press, 1965.

Aldred, Cyril:
Egyptian Art: In the Days of the Pharaohs 3100-320 BC London: Thames and Hudson, 1980.
The Egyptians. London: Thames and Hudson, 1984.

Allchin, Bridget, and Raymond Allchin, *The Rise of Civilization in India and Pakistan.* New York: Cambridge University Press, 1982.

Asthana, Shashi, *History and Archaeology of India's Contacts with Other Countries: From Earliest Times to 300 B.C.* Delhi: B. R. Publishing, 1976.

Atkinson, R.J.C., *Stonehenge.* Harmondsworth, England: Penguin Books, 1979.

Baines, John, and Jaromír Málek, *Atlas of Ancient Egypt.* New York: Facts on File, 1984.

Basham, A. L., *The Wonder That Was India: A Study of the History and Culture of the Indian Sub-Continent before the Coming of the Muslims.* New York: Hawthorn Books, 1963.

Beckerath, Jürgen von, *Handbuch der Ägyptischen Königsnamen.* Munich: Deutscher Kunstverlag, 1984.

Billard, Jules B., ed., *Ancient Egypt: Discovering Its Splendors.* Washington, D.C.: National Geographic Society, 1978.

Blunden, Caroline, and Mark Elvin, *Cultural Atlas of China.* New York: Facts on File, 1983.

Boorstin, Daniel J., *The Discoverers.* New York: Random House, 1983.

Branigan, K., ed., *The Atlas of Archaeology.* New York: St. Martin's Press, 1982.

Breasted, James Henry, *Ancient Records of Egypt.* Chicago: University of Chicago Press, 1906.

Brennan, Martin, *The Boyne Valley Vision.* Portlaoise, Ireland: Dolmen Press, 1980.

British Museum, Department of Egyptian Antiquities, *An Introduction to Ancient Egypt.* New York: Farrar Straus Giroux, 1979.

Brown, Ann, *Arthur Evans and the Palace of Minos.* Oxford: Ashmolean Museum, 1983.

Bulfinch, Thomas, *Bulfinch's Mythology.* New York: Thomas Y. Crowell, 1970.

Casson, Lionel, *The Ancient Mariners: Seafarers and Sea Fighters of the Mediterranean in Ancient Times.* New York: Macmillan, 1959.

Casson, Lionel, and the Editors of Time-Life Books, *Ancient Egypt* (Great Ages of Man series). Alexandria, Virginia: Time-Life Books, 1965.

Cavendish, Richard, *Prehistoric England.* New York: British Heritage Press, 1983.

Ceram, C. W., *Gods, Graves, and Scholars: The Story of Archaeology.* New York: Bantam Books, 1967.

Chang, Kwang-Chih:
The Archaeology of Ancient China. New Haven: Yale University Press, 1977.
Art, Myth, and Ritual: The Path to Political Authority in Ancient China. Cambridge, Massachusetts: Harvard University Press, 1983.
Shang Civilization. New Haven: Yale University Press, 1980.

Chippindale, Christopher, *Stonehenge Complete.* London: Thames and Hudson, 1983.

Christopoulos, George A., ed., *Prehistory and Protohistory.* Vol. 1 of *History of the Hellenic World.* University Park: Pennsylvania State University Press, 1974.

Claiborne, Robert, and the Editors of Time-Life Books, *The Birth of Writing* (The Emergence of Man series). New York: Time-Life Books, 1974.

Coffey, George, *New Grange and Other Incised Tumuli in Ireland.* Dorset, England: Dolphin Press, 1977.

Cottrell, Leonard, *The Bull of Minos.* London: Pan Books, 1955.

Davaras, Costis, *Guide to Cretan Antiquities.* Park Ridge, New Jersey: Noyes Press, 1976.

Delaporte, L., *Mesopotamia: The Babylonian and Assyrian Civilization.* New York: Alfred A. Knopf, 1925.

Diringer, David, *The Book before Printing: Ancient, Medieval and Oriental.* New York: Dover Publications, 1982.

Doumas, Christos G., *Thera: Pompeii of the Ancient Aegean.* London: Thames and Hudson, 1983.

Edwards, I.E.S., *The Pyramids of Egypt.* New York: Penguin Books, 1985.

Edwards, I.E.S., C. J. Gadd, N.G.L. Hammond, and E. Sollberger, *The Cambridge Ancient History,* Vol. 2, Part 1. Cambridge: Cambridge University Press, 1973.

Emery, Walter B., *Lost Land Emerging.* New York: Charles Scribner's Sons, 1967.

Erman, Adolf, *Life in Ancient Egypt.* Transl. by H. M. Tirard. New York: Dover Publications, 1971.

Evans, Sir Arthur J., *The Palace of Minos at Knossos.* 4 vols. London: Macmillan, 1921-1935.

Evans, J. D.:
Ancient Peoples and Places: Malta. London: Thames and Hudson, 1959.
The Prehistoric Antiquities of the Maltese Islands: A Survey. London: Athlone Press, 1971.

Firth, Cecil M., and J. E. Quibell, *The Step Pyramid.* Vols. 1 and 2 of *Excavations at Saqqara.* Cairo: Imprimerie de l'Institut Français d'Archéologie Orientale, 1935 – 1936.

Frankfort, Henri:
Ancient Egyptian Religion: An Interpretation. New York: Harper & Row, 1961.
The Art and Architecture of the Ancient Orient. New York: Penguin Books, 1970.

Gardiner, Sir Alan:
Egypt of the Pharaohs: An Introduction. New York: Oxford University Press, 1961.
Egyptian Grammar: Being an Introduction to the Study of Hieroglyphs. Oxford: Ashmolean Museum, 1979.

Gaur, Albertine, *A History of Writing.* London: British Library, 1984.

Glotz, Gustave, *The Aegean Civilization.* New York: Alfred A. Knopf, 1925.

Glubok, Shirley, ed., *Discovering the Royal Tombs at Ur.* Abridged and adapted from *Ur Excavations: The Royal Cemetery* by C. Leonard Woolley. New York: Macmillan, 1969.

Hadingham, Evan, *Circles and Standing Stones: An Illustrated Exploration of Megalith Mysteries of Early Britain.* New York: Walker, 1975.

Hägg, Robin, and Nanno Marinatos, eds., *The Minoan Thalassocracy: Myth and Reality.* Stockholm: Swedish Institute in Athens, 1984.

Hallo, William W., and William Kelly Simpson, *The Ancient Near East.* New York: Harcourt Brace Jovanovich, 1971.

Hamblin, Dora Jane, and the Editors of Time-Life Books, *The First Cities* (The Emergence of Man series). New York: Time-Life Books, 1973.

Harris, Roy, *The Origin of Writing.* London: Gerald Duckworth, 1986.

Hart, George, *A Dictionary of Egyptian Gods and Goddesses.* Boston: Routledge & Kegan Paul, 1986.

Hawkes, Jacquetta, and Sir Leonard Woolley, *History of Mankind: Prehistory and the Beginnings of Civilization.* New York: Harper & Row, 1963.

Ho, Ping-Ti, *The Cradle of the East.* Hong Kong: Chinese University of Hong Kong, 1975.

Homer, *The Iliad.* Transl. by Richmond Lattimore. Chicago: University of Chicago Press, 1951.

Hood, Sinclair, and David Smyth, *Archaeological Survey of the Knossos Area.* Suppl. Vol. 14. [London]: British School at Athens, 1981.

Hood, Sinclair, and William Taylor, *The Bronze Age Palace at Knossos.* Suppl. Vol. 13. [London]: British School at Athens, 1981.

Hutchinson, R. W., *Prehistoric Crete.* Baltimore: Penguin Books, 1962.

Institute of Archaeology, Academy of Social Sciences, People's Republic of China, *Recent Archaeological Discoveries in the People's Republic of China.* Paris: UNESCO, 1984.

Jacobsen, Thorkild, *Toward the Image of Tammuz and Other Essays on Mesopotamian History and Culture.* Ed. by William L. Moran. Cambridge: Harvard University Press, 1970.

Jansen, Michael, *Die Indus-Zivilisation.* Cologne: DuMont, 1986.

Jenkins, Nancy, *The Boat beneath the Pyramid: King Cheops' Royal Ship.* London: Thames and Hudson, 1980.

Katan, Norma Jean, with Barbara Mintz, *Hieroglyphs: The Writing of Ancient Egypt.* London: British Museum, 1985.

Knauth, Percy, and the Editors of Time-Life Books, *The Metalsmiths* (The Emergence of Man series). New York: Time-Life Books, 1974.

Kramer, Samuel Noah:
History Begins at Sumer. Philadelphia: University of Pennsylvania Press, 1981.
The Sumerians: Their History, Culture, and Character. Chicago: University of Chicago Press, 1963.

Kramer, Samuel Noah, and the Editors of Time-Life Books, *Cradle of Civilization* (Great Ages of Man series). New York: Time-Life Books, 1967.

Lauer, Jean-Philippe:
La Pyramide à Degrés: L'Architecture. Cairo: Imprimerie de l'Institut Français, d'Archéologie Orientale, 1936.
Saqqara: The Royal Cemetery of Memphis. London: Thames and Hudson, 1976.

Lloyd, Seton, *The Archaeology of Mesopotamia: From the Old Stone Age to the Persian Conquest.* London: Thames and Hudson, 1978.

Lurker, Manfred, *The Gods and Symbols of Ancient Egypt.* London: Thames and Hudson, 1980.

MacKie, Euan, *The Megalith Builders.* Oxford: Phaidon Press, 1977.

McNeill, William H.:
The Rise of the West: A History of the Human Community. Chicago: University of Chicago Press, 1963.
A World History. New York: Oxford University Press, 1979.

Mahajan, Vidya Dhar, *Ancient India.* Delhi: S. Chand, 1968.

Málek, Jaromír, *In the Shadow of the Pyramid: Egypt during the Old Kingdom.* London: Orbis, 1986.

Mallowan, M.E.L., *Early Mesopotamia and Iran.* New York: McGraw-Hill, 1965.

Marshall, Sir John, *Mohenjo-daro and the Indus Civilization.* Delhi: Indological Book House, 1973.

Mellersh, H.E.L., *Minoan Crete.* New York: G. P. Putnam's Sons, 1967.

Mendelssohn, Kurt, *The Riddle of the Pyramids.* New York: Praeger, 1974.

Michalowski, Kazimierz, *Art of Ancient Egypt.* New York: Harry N. Abrams, 1985.

Möller, Georg, *Hieratische Paläographie.* Osnabrück, Germany: Otto Zeller, 1965.

Moore, R. I., ed., *Rand McNally Atlas of World History.* Chicago: Rand McNally, 1983.

Moorey, P.R.S., *Ur 'of the Chaldees': A Revised and Updated Edition of Sir Leonard Woolley's Excavations at Ur.* Ithaca: Cornell University Press, 1982.

Mughal, Mohammad Rafique, *The Early Harappan Period in the Greater Indus Valley and Northern Baluchistan: A Dissertation in Anthropology.* Philadelphia: University of Pennsylvania, 1970.

Murray, Margaret A., *The Splendor That Was Egypt.* New York: Hawthorn Books, 1963.

Newby, P. H., *The Egypt Story: Its Art, Its Monuments, Its People, Its History.* New York: Abbeville Press, no date.

Niemeier, Wolf-Dietrich, *Die Palaststilkeramik von Knossos.* Berlin: Gebr. Mann, 1985.

Oates, Joan, *Babylon.* London: Thames and Hudson, 1979.

Ogden, Jack, *Jewellery of the Ancient World.* New York: Rizzoli, 1982.

O'Kelly, Michael J., *Newgrange: Archaeology, Art and Legend.* London: Thames and Hudson, 1982.

Oppenheim, A. Leo, *Ancient Mesopotamia: Portrait of a Dead Civilization.* Chicago: University of Chicago Press, 1977.

Parrot, André, *Sumer.* Paris: Gallimard, 1981.

Pendlebury, J.D.S.:
The Archaeology of Crete: An Introduction. New York: Biblo and Tannen, 1963.
A Handbook to the Palace of Minos at Knossos. Chicago: Ares, 1979.

Piggott, Stuart, *Prehistoric India to 1000 B.C.* London: Cassell, 1962.

Platon, Nicholas, *Zakros: The Discovery of a Lost Palace of Ancient Greece.* New York: Charles Scribner's Sons, 1971.

Poss, John R., *Stones of Destiny: Keystones of Civilization.* Houghton, Michigan: Michigan Technological University, 1975.

Possehl, Gregory L., ed., *Harappan Civilization: A Contemporary Perspective.* New Delhi: Oxford & Ibh Publishing, 1982.

Postgate, Nicholas, *The First Empire* (The Making of the Past). Oxford: Phaidon Press, 1977.

Randhawa, M. S., *A History of Agriculture in India.* Vol. 1. New Delhi: Indian Council of Agricultural Research, 1980.

Raymond, Robert, *Out of the Fiery Furnace: The Impact of Metals on the History of Mankind.* University Park: Pennsylvania State University Press, 1986.

Redman, Charles L., *The Rise of Civilization: From Early Farmers to Urban Society in the Ancient Near East.* San Francisco: W. H. Freeman, 1978.

Roebuck, Carl, *The World of Ancient Times.* New York: Charles Scribner's Sons, 1966.

Salonen, Armas, *Agricultura Mesopotamica.* Helsinki: Suomalaisen Kirjallisuuden Kirjapaino Oy, 1968.

Sampson, Geoffrey, *Writing Systems: A Linguistic Introduction.* London: Hutchinson, 1985.

Sandars, N. K., *The Epic of Gilgamesh.* Baltimore: Penguin Books, 1964.

Smith, H. S., *Excavations.* Vol. 1 of *The Fortress of Buhen.* London: Egypt Exploration Society, 1976.

Smith, W. Stevenson, *The Art and Architecture of Ancient Egypt.* New York: Penguin Books, 1984.

Spencer, A. J., *Death in Ancient Egypt.* New York: Penguin Books, 1984.

Steinhardt, Nancy Shatzman, *Chinese Traditional Architecture.* New York: China Institute in America, 1984.

Strommenger, Eva, *Ur.* Munich: Hirmer, 1964.

Stuart, George E., ed., *Peoples and Places of the Past.* Washington, D.C.: National Geographic Society, 1983.

Thomas, Hugh, *A History of the World.* New York: Harper & Row, 1982.

Trigger, B. G., B. J. Kemp, D. O'Connor, and A. B. Lloyd, *Ancient Egypt: A Social History.* Cambridge: Cambridge University Press, 1983.

Watson, William, *Early Civilization in China.* New York: McGraw-Hill, 1966.

Wernick, Robert, and the Editors of Time-Life Books, *The Monument Builders* (The Emergence of Man series). New York: Time-Life Books, 1973.

Wheeler, Sir Mortimer, *The Indus Civilization.* New York: Cambridge University Press, 1968.

White, J. E. Manchip, *Ancient Egypt.* New York: Thomas Y. Crowell, 1953.

White, Joyce C., *Ban Chiang: Discovery of a Lost Bronze Age.* Philadelphia: University Museum, University of Pennsylvania and Washington, D.C.: Smithsonian Institution Traveling Exhibition Service, 1982.

Winlock, H. E., *Excavations at Deir El Bahri: 1911-1931.* New York: Macmillan, 1942.

Wolkstein, Diane, and Samuel Noah Kramer, *Inanna: Queen of Heaven and Earth: Her Stories and Hymns from Sumer.* New York: Harper & Row, 1983.

Wolpert, Stanley, *A New History of India.* New York: Oxford University Press, 1982.

Woolley, Sir Leonard:
The Sumerians. New York: W. W. Norton, 1965.
Ur Excavations:
Vol. 5, *The Ziggurat and Its Surroundings.* London: Oxford University Press for the Joint Expedition of the British Museum and of the University Museum, University of Pennsylvania, Philadelphia, to Mesopotamia, 1939.
Vol. 6, *The Buildings of the Third Dynasty.* London: Oxford University Press for the Joint Expedition of the British Museum and of the University Museum, University of Pennsylvania, Philadelphia, to Mesopotamia, 1974.

PERIODICALS

Chang, K. C., "In Search of China's Beginnings: New Light on an Old Civilization," *American Scientist* (New Haven), March-April 1981.

Jansen, Michael, "Mohenjo-daro, City of the Indus Valley." *Endeavour* (Great Britain), Vol. 9, No. 4, 1985.

Jasim, Sabah Abboud, and Joan Oates, "Early Tokens and Tablets in Mesopotamia: New Information from Tell Abada and Tell Brak." *World Archaeology* (London), February 1986.

Olivier, J.-P., "Cretan Writing in the Second Millennium B.C." *World Archaeology* (London), February 1986.

Ray, John D., "The Emergence of Writing in Egypt." *World Archaeology* (London), February 1986.

Shaw, Joseph W.:
"Evidence for the Minoan Tripartite Shrine." *American Journal of Archaeology 82,* 1978.
"Excavations at Kommos (Crete) during 1984-1985." *Hesperia* (Athens), July-September 1986.

Urban, Gunter, and Michael Jansen:
"Interim Reports Vol. 1: Reports on Field Work Carried Out at Mohenjo-daro." *German Research Project* (Aachen), 1982-83.
"Mohenjo-daro: Dokumentation in der Archäologie." *Forschungsprojekt DFG* (Aachen), 1983.
"The Resurrection of the Hill of the Dead: Discovery of a City on the Indus." *German Research; Reports of the DFG* (Bonn), 1985.

Young, Gavin, "Water Dwellers in a Desert World." *National Geographic* (Washington, D.C.), April 1976.

OTHER

Daniel, Glyn, and Poul Kjaerum, eds., "Megalithic Graves and Ritual." Papers presented at the III Atlantic Colloquium, Moesgard, Denmark, 1969.

INDEX

ACKNOWLEDGMENTS

The editors wish to thank the following individuals and institutions for their valuable assistance in the preparation of this volume:

Crete: Herakleion — J. Sakellarakis, Ephor of Antiquities for Eastern Crete and Director of Herakleion Museum. Rethymnon — Daphne Gondicas, Loutra.

England: Banbury, Oxfordshire — Gerald Cadogan. Cambridge — David Trump, Staff Tutor in Archaeology, Board of Extra-Mural Studies, University of Cambridge. London — Carol Andrews, Department of Egyptian Antiquities, British Museum; I. L. Finkel, Department of Western Asiatic Antiquities, British Museum; Seton Lloyd, Professor Emeritus of Western Asiatic Archaeology, University of London; Anne Millard; Brian A. Tremain, Photographic Services, British Museum. Manchester — William C. Brice. Sheffield — Keith Branigan, Department of Archaeology and Prehistory, University of Sheffield. Oxford — Ann Brown, Ashmolean Museum; Michael Vickers, Department of Antiquities, Ashmolean Museum; Sinclair Hood.

Federal Republic of Germany: Aachen — Günter Urban, Präsident, Gesellschaft zur Förderung der Forschung in Süd-Asien, RWTH. Berlin — Joachim S. Karig, Ägyptisches Museum, Staatliche Museen Preussischer Kulturbesitz; Heidi Klein, Bildarchiv Preussischer Kulturbesitz; Hans Nissen, Institut für Archaeologie, Freie Universität; Jürgen Settgast, Direktor, Ägyptisches Museum, Staatliche Museen Preussischer Kulturbesitz; Eva Strommenger, Museum für Vor- und Frühgeschichte, Staatliche Museen Preussischer Kulturbesitz; Marianne Yaldiz, Museum für Indische Kunst, Staatliche Museen Preussischer Kulturbesitz. Bonn — Hanno Beck, Geographisches Institut, Universität Bonn; Stephan Seidlmeyer, Ägyptologisches Institut, Universität Bonn; Jürgen Using, Direktor, Ägyptologisches Institut, Universität Bonn. Hildesheim — Bettina Schmitz, Roemer und Pelizaeus Museum. Mainz — Ludwig Kirsch, Philipp von Zabern Verlag. Munich — Irmgard Ernstmeier, Hirmer Verlag; Dietrich Wildung, Direktor, Staatliche Sammlung Ägyptische Kunst.

France: Paris — Marie-France Aubert, Conservateur au Département des Antiquités Égyptiennes, Musée du Louvre; François Avril, Curateur, Département des Manuscrits, Bibliothèque Nationale; Laure Beaumont-Maillet, Conservateur en Chef du Cabinet des Estampes, Bibliothèque Nationale; Catherine Bélanger, Chargée des Relations Extérieures du Musée du Louvre; Jeannette Chalufour, Archives Tallandier; Béatrice Coti, Directrice du Service Iconographique, Éditions Mazenod; Antoinette Decaudin, Documentaliste, Département des Antiquités Orientales, Musée du Louvre; Michel Dewachter, Attaché au Cabinet d'Égyptologie du Collège de France; Michel Fleury, Président de la IV Section de l'École Pratique des Hautes Études; Françoise Jestaz, Conservateur, Cabinet des Estampes, Bibliothèque Nationale; Claudine Lanoir, Conférencière, Service de Muséologie et d'Action Culturelle, Musée du Louvre; Marie Montembault, Documentaliste, Département des Antiquités Grecques et Romaines, Musée du Louvre; Marie-Odile Roy, Service Photographique, Bibliothèque Nationale; Jacqueline Sanson, Conservateur, Directeur du Service Photographique, Bibliothèque Nationale.

German Democratic Republic: Berlin — Liane Jakob-Rost, Direktor, Vorderasiatisches Museum, Staatliche Museen zu Berlin; Hannelore Kischewitz, Ägyptisches Museum, Staatliche Museen zu Berlin; Evelyn Klengel-Brandt, Vorderasiatisches Museum, Staatliche Museen zu Berlin; Wolfgang Müller, Direktor, Ägyptisches Museum, Staatliche Museen zu Berlin.

Greece: Athens — John C. Bastias, Director, Ekdotike Athenon; Robin Hagg, Director, Swedish Institute in Athens; T. A. MacGillivray, Assistant Director, British School of Archaeology at Athens; Nanno Marinatos, Swedish Institute in Athens.

Italy: Antella — Ancilla Antonini, Scala. Milan — Luisa Ricciarini, Agenzia Ricciarini.

Scotland: Glasgow — Euan W. MacKie, Department of Archaeology and Anthropology, Hunterian Museum.

U.S.A.: Connecticut: New Haven — David Goodrich. Maryland: Fort Washington — Melva M. Holloman. Massachusetts: Cambridge — K. C. Chang, Department of Anthropology, Peabody Museum, Harvard University. Pennsylvania: Philadelphia — Heather Peters, The University Museum, University of Pennsylvania. Tennessee: Nashville — Linda DiCiaula, American Association for State and Local History.

The index for this volume was prepared by Roy Nanovic.

PICTURE CREDITS

Bull's-head lyre, from the royal tombs of Ur, wood, shell, and gold with lapis lazuli, Sumerian, c. 2500 BC, The University Museum, University of Pennsylvania (Robert Lautman). **28, 29:** Gaming board, wood with squares of shell, lapis lazuli, and red limestone set in bitumen, Sumerian, c. 2500 BC, Trustees of the British Museum, London, WA 120834 — Hounds and Jackals game, ivory, Egyptian, Twelfth Dynasty, c. 1801-1792 BC, The Metropolitan Museum of Art, Excavations of The Metropolitan Museum of Art, 1915-1916, the Carnarvon Collection, Gift of Edward S. Harkness, 1926 (26.7.1287); Game board and throwing sticks of wood, blue faience, and ivory, Egyptian, Eighteenth Dynasty, c. 1450-1360 BC, The Metropolitan Museum of Art, Rogers Fund, 1912 and 1919, New York (12.182.72-19.2.2.19.27). View #3). **30:** The Standard of Ur, mosaic of shell, lapis lazuli, and red limestone in bitumen, royal cemetery, Ur, c. 2500 BC, Trustees of the British Museum, London, WA 121201. **33:** The Vulture Stela, stone, Sumerian, c. 2500-2000 BC, Musée du Louvre, Paris (G. Dagli Orti, Paris); Stela of Naram-Sin, limestone, Akkadian, c. 2250 BC, Musée du Louvre/Réunion des Musées Nationaux, Paris. **34:** Bust of King Sargon, bronze, Akkadian, c. 2300 BC, Iraq Museum, Baghdad (Claus Hansmann, Stockdorf). **37:** Cuneiform inscription, clay, Sumerian, c. 2100 BC, Musée du Louvre/© Cliché Musées Nationaux, Paris. **38:** Accounting tablet, clay, Sumerian, c. 3000 BC, Ashmolean Museum, Oxford, 1926.564 (Michael Freeman); Chart illustrating the development of Sumerian language by Frederic E. Bigio from B-C Graphics, based on information supplied by consultant, I. L. Finkel, London. **39:** Legal document and envelope, clay, Akkadian, c. 1800-1700 BC, Trustees of the British Museum, London, WA 131449a; Accounting tablet, clay, Sumerian, c. 2350 BC, Musée du Louvre, Paris (Bulloz, Paris) — Messenger text, clay, Sumerian, c. 2100 BC, Trustees of the British Museum, London, WA 105616. **40:** Model of a sheep's liver, clay, Akkadian, c. 1900-1800 BC, Musée du Louvre, Paris (Bulloz, Paris) — Fragment, Akkadian language mathematical text, clay, Babylonian, c. 1700 BC, Trustees of the British Museum, London, WA 15285. **41:** Medical text, clay, Sumerian, c. 2100 BC, The University Museum, University of Pennsylvania — Duck weight, diorite, Sumerian, c. 2050 BC, National Museum, Baghdad (Claus Hansmann, Stockdorf). **42:** Statue of King Gudea of Lagash, calcite, Sumerian, c. 2150 BC, Musée du Louvre, Paris (F. Simion/Ricciarini, Milan); Figurine, copper, Sumerian, c. 2100 BC, Trustees of the British Museum, London WA 113896. **43:** Architectural cone, clay, Sumerian, c. 2150 BC, Trustees of the British Museum, London, WA 117837; The Weld-Blundell prism, clay, Sumerian, c. 1827-1817 BC, Ashmolean Museum, Oxford, 1923.444 (Michael Freeman). **44, 45:**

Flood Tablet II, clay, Babylonian, c. 1700 BC, Trustees of the British Museum, London, WA 78942+; Detail, Hammurabi's Code, black basalt, Babylonian, post-1800 BC, Musée du Louvre, Paris (Dmitri Kessel, Paris) — Stela of Hammurabi's Code of Law, black basalt, Babylonian, post-1800 BC, Musée du Louvre, Paris (Dmitri Kessel, Paris). **46:** Chart illustrating the development of Egyptian language by John Drummond, based on information supplied by consultant, Christophe Barbotin, Paris; "Eternity" hieroglyph, Egyptian (Jean Vertut, Paris). **47:** Detail, Rhind mathematical papyrus, black and red ink, Egyptian, c. 1650 BC, Trustees of the British Museum, London, EA 10057; Royal scribe, carved wood, Egyptian, Third Dynasty, c. 2686-2613 BC, Egyptian National Museum, Cairo (Kodansha Ltd., Tokyo). **48, 49:** Sallier papyrus 2, black and red ink, Egyptian, Twelfth Dynasty, c. 1994-1781 BC, Trustees of the British Museum, London, EA 10182/2 — Scribe's penholder, Egyptian, Ashmolean Museum, Oxford, E1989 (Gordon Roberton). **50, 51:** Chamber of Sen-nefer's tomb, Egyptian, Eighteenth Dynasty, c. 1550-1291 BC (Jean Bovot-Kurz, Cliché Établi pour la Reconstruction Photographique le Tombe Sen-nefer); Stela of Prince Netcher-Aperaf, clay, Egyptian, Fourth Dynasty, c. 2600-2475 BC, Egyptian National Museum, Cairo (John G. Ross, Rome). **52, 53:** Book of the Dead, ink on papyrus, Egyptian, Eighteenth Dynasty, c. 1550-1291 BC, Musée du Louvre, Paris/© Cliché Musées Nationaux, Paris — Book of the Dead, ink on papyrus, Egyptian, Eleventh Dynasty, c. 2000 BC, Staatliche Museen zu Berlin, Hauptstadt der DDR, Papyrussammlung P 10 477 (Scala from Art Resource, New York). **54:** Menkaure triad, slate, Egyptian, Fourth Dynasty, c. 2500 BC, Egyptian National Museum, Cairo (John G. Ross, Rome). **56:** Map of Egypt, drawn by Carol Schwartz of Stansbury, Ronsaville, Wood Inc. **57:** Detail, bas-relief of boating on the Nile, Egyptian, Fifth Dynasty, c. 2400 BC (© Brian Brake from Photo Researchers). **58, 59:** Hedgehog statuette, faience, Egyptian, Twelfth Dynasty, c. 1800 BC, Ägyptisches Museum, SMPK Berlin (West) (Margarete Büsing); Bas-relief of hippopotamus hunters, Egyptian, Fifth Dynasty, 2475-2345 BC, Ägyptisches Museum, SMPK Berlin (West) (Margarete Büsing); Statuette of crocodile god, bronze and gold, Egyptian, Twelfth Dynasty, c. 1800 BC (Staatliche Sammlung Ägyptischer Kunst, Munich) — Statuette of hippopotamus, faience, Egyptian, Twelfth Dynasty, c. 1800 BC, Ägyptisches Museum, SMPK, Berlin (West) (Margarete Büsing). **61:** Narmer palette, slate, Egyp-

tian, First Dynasty, 3000-2820 BC, Egyptian National Museum, Cairo (Jean Vertut, from *L'Art de l'Ancienne Egypte*, Éditions Mazenod, Paris, 1968). **62, 63:** Detail, *heb sed* chapels, Saqqara, art by Lana Rigsby, Lowell Williams Design, Inc., based on a reconstruction by Jean-Philippe Lauer — Necropolis of King Djoser, Saqqara, art by Lana Rigsby, Lowell Williams Design, Inc., based on reconstruction by Jean-Philippe Lauer. **65:** Statue of seated scribe, painted limestone, Egyptian, Fourth Dynasty, c. 2500 BC, Musée du Louvre, Paris (Scala, Florence). **66:** Detail, bas-relief of papyrus making, Egyptian, Fifth Dynasty, 2475-2345 BC (G. Dagli Orti, Paris) — Relief of Thoth, god of writing, Egyptian, Fifth-Sixth Dynasty, 2475-2195 BC (C.d.A. Jacqueline Guillot from Edimedia, Paris. Droits Reserves) — Detail, painted relief of harvesting papyrus, Egyptian, Fifth Dynasty, c. 2400 BC, Papyrus Institute, Cairo (G. Dagli Orti, Paris). **68:** Detail, bas-relief of shipbuilders, Egyptian, Fifth Dynasty, 2475-2345 BC (G. Dagli Orti, Paris). **69:** Detail, bas-relief of sculptors, Egyptian, Fifth Dynasty, 2475-2345 BC (Giraudon, Paris). **70:** Egyptian official's courtyard, art by Greg Harlin of Stansbury, Ronsaville, Wood Inc. **72, 73:** Model of scribes inventorying cattle, painted wood, Egyptian, Eleventh Dynasty, c. 2000 BC, Egyptian National Museum, Cairo (Jürgen Liepe, Berlin (West)/Verlag Philipp von Zabern, Mainz). **74:** Detail, wall painting of ritual slaughter, tempera, Egyptian, Sixth Dynasty, c. 2200 BC, Museo Egizio, Turin (Nimatallah/Ricciarini, Milan) — Detail, relief of cow milking, limestone, Egyptian, Egyptian National Museum, Cairo (Walter Rawlings from Robert Harding Picture Library, London) — Detail, bas-relief of fishing scene, Egyptian, Sixth Dynasty, 2345-2195 BC (Giraudon, Paris). **75:** Model of woman filtering beer, painted limestone, Egyptian, Fifth Dynasty, 2475-2345 BC, Museo Archeologico, Florence (Scala, Florence) — Model of woman grinding grain, painted limestone, Egyptian, Fifth Dynasty, 2475-2345 BC, Museo Archeologico, Florence (Scala, Florence). **76:** Detail, stela of steward Montuwosre, painted limestone, Egyptian, Twelfth Dynasty, c. 1955 BC, The Metropolitan Museum of Art, Gift of Edward S. Harkness, 1912 (12.184); Detail, painted relief of offering bearers, Egyptian, Fifth Dynasty, 2475-2345 BC (Fred J. Maroon). **78:** Statue of Khephren, diorite, Egyptian, Fourth Dynasty, c. 2525 BC, Egyptian National Museum, Cairo (G. Dagli Orti, Paris). **80, 81:** Great Sphinx at Giza, art by Rob Wood of Stansbury, Ronsaville, Wood Inc. **83:** West Barbican, Buhen, art by Lana Rigsby, Lowell Williams Design, Inc., based on an illustration by Walter B. Emery. **84, 85:** Fortress of Buhen, art by Frederic F. Bigio from B-C Graphics, based on a diagram by Walter B. Emery — West wall, inner

stronghold, Buhen, art by Lana Rigsby, Lowell Williams Design, Inc., based on an illustration by Walter B. Emery. **87:** Detail, royal cemetery, Ur, art by Greg Harlin of Stansbury, Ronsaville, Wood Inc. **88, 89:** Royal cemetery, Ur, art by Greg Harlin of Stansbury, Ronsaville, Wood Inc. **90, 91:** Royal cemetery, Ur, art by Greg Harlin of Stansbury, Ronsaville, Wood Inc. **92, 93:** Burial of Khufu, Giza, art by Greg Harlin of Stansbury, Ronsaville, Wood Inc. **94, 95:** Burial of Khufu, Giza, art by Rob Wood of Stansbury, Ronsaville, Wood Inc.; inset, cross-section of Great Pyramid, Giza, art by Rob Wood of Stansbury, Ronsaville, Wood Inc. **96:** Fresco of dolphins, Minoan, c. 1600 BC, Herakleion Museum, Crete (Ekdotike Athenon, Athens). **99:** Map of northeastern Mediterranean, drawn by Carol Schwartz of Stansbury, Ronsaville, Wood Inc. **100:** Seated figurine with cup, marble, Cyclades islands, Greece, c. 2800-2300 BC, N. P. Goulandris Collection, Museum of Cycladic and Ancient Greek Art, Athens (Nikos Kontos, Athens); Figurine of pregnant female, Cyclades islands, Greece, c. 2800-2300 BC (Scala from Art Resource, New York); Seated harp player, marble, Cyclades islands, Greece, c. 2400-2200 BC, National Archeological Museum, Athens (Luisa Ricciarini, Milan). **102, 103:** Harbor at Kommos, Crete, art by Greg Harlin of Stansbury, Ronsaville, Wood Inc., based on drawings by Giuliana Bianco and Joseph W. Shaw. **106, 107:** The palace of Minos at Knossos, art by Rob Wood of Stansbury, Ronsaville, Wood Inc., based on drawings by Sinclair Hood, William Taylor, David Smyth, and Nikos Gouvoussis. **108:** Tablet of business transaction, clay, Minoan, c. 1450 BC, Herakleion Museum, Crete (Ekdotike Athenon, Athens). **111:** The throne room in the palace of Minos at Knossos, art by Lana Rigsby, Lowell Williams Design, Inc., based on information from "New Restorations of Minoan Frescoes from Knossos," M.A.S. Cameron and *Das Thronraumareal des Palastes von Knossos*, S. Mirié, 1979. **112:** The Lily Prince, fresco, Minoan, c. 1600-1550 BC, Herakleion Museum, Crete (© Emilio-F. Simion/Ricciarini, Milan); *Monkey Scrambling over Rocks*, fresco, Minoan, c. 2000-1700 BC (Michos Tzovaras from Art Resource, New York) — The Antelopes, fresco, Minoan, c. 1500 BC, National Archeological Museum, Athens (Ekdotike Athenon, Athens); *The Fisherman with Mackerel*, fresco, Minoan, c. 1500 BC, National Archeological Museum, Athens (Ekdotike Athenon, Athens). **113:** *Boxing Children*, fresco, Minoan, c. 1500 BC, National Archeological Museum, Athens (Scala, Florence); *The Bull Dancers,* fresco, Minoan, c. 1500 BC, Herakleion Museum, Crete (Scala, Florence) — Detail, frieze of Theran ships, fresco, Minoan, c. 1500 BC, National Archeological Museum, Athens (Ekdotike Athenon, Athens) — Detail, *The House of Ladies,* fresco, Minoan, c. 1500 BC, National Archeological Museum, Athens (Scala, Florence); Lilies and swallows, fresco, Minoan, c. 1500 BC, National Archeological Museum, Athens (Scala, Florence); *The Young Priestess,* fresco, Minoan, c. 1500 BC, National Archeological Museum, Athens (Ekdotike Athenon, Athens). **114:** Bull's-head libation vessel, black steatite, gilded wood, painted rock crystal, and shell, Minoan, c. 1550-1500 BC, Herakleion Museum, Crete (Ekdotike Athenon, Athens). **115:** Plaque of a cow and her calf, faience, Minoan, c. 1600 BC, Ashmolean Museum, Oxford, AE 1123 (Michael Freeman). **116:** Double ax, gold, Minoan, c. 1600 BC, Herakleion Museum, Crete (Ekdotike Athenon, Athens). **117:** Statuette of a snake goddess, faience, Minoan, c. 1600 BC, Ashmolean Museum, Oxford, AE 1114 (Michael Freeman). **119:** Shrine at Kato Zakros, art by Lana Rigsby, Lowell Williams Design, Inc., based on a drawing by Giuliana Bianco and Joseph W. Shaw. **121:** Detail, megalith, art by Rob Wood of Stansbury, Ronsaville, Wood Inc. **122, 123:** Stonehenge, England, art by Rob Wood of Stansbury, Ronsaville, Wood Inc. **124, 125:** New Grange, Ireland, art by Carol Schwartz of Stansbury, Ronsaville, Wood Inc. **126, 127:** Ggantija, Malta, art by Rob Wood of Stansbury, Ronsaville, Wood Inc. **128:** Bust of priest-king, Mohenjo-daro, steatite, Harappan, c. 2100-1750 BC, National Museum of Pakistan, Karachi/© Municipality of Aachen (G. Helmes, Aachen). **131:** Map of Asia, drawn by Rob Wood of Stansbury, Ronsaville, Wood Inc. **132:** Street scene, Mohenjo-daro, art by Greg Harlin of Stansbury, Ronsaville, Wood Inc., based on a drawing by Rolf Bunse. **136, 137:** Mohenjo-daro, art by Rob Wood of Stansbury, Ronsaville, Wood Inc., based on a drawing by Rolf Bunse. **139:** Bathing area, Mohenjo-daro, art by Greg Harlin of Stansbury, Ronsaville, Wood Inc., based on a drawing by Rolf Bunse. **140:** Seal of zebu bull, steatite, Harappan, c. 2300-1750 BC, Karachi Museum, Pakistan (Robert Harding Picture Library, Ltd., London) — Seal of "unicorn," steatite, Harappan, c. 2300-1750 BC (S.H.J. Zaidi from Robert Harding Picture Library, Ltd., London) — Seal of rhinoceros, steatite, Harappan, c. 2300-1750 BC, Karachi Museum, Pakistan (Robert Harding Picture Library, Ltd., London) — Impression, seal of elephant, original seal of steatite, Harappan, c. 2300-1750 BC (Emmett Bright, Rome). **142, 143:** Ma-tch'ang style vase, terra-cotta, Chinese, c. 2000-1500 BC, Asian Art Museum, San Francisco (Jean Mazenod, from *L'Art de l'Ancienne Chine,* Éditions Mazenod, Paris) — Burial pots, ceramic, Ban Chiang, Thai-

land, c. 3600-1000 BC, The University Museum, University of Pennsylvania(3); Jar lid, Harappan, c. 3000-2000 BC, New Delhi National Museum, India (C.B.O.-Giraudon, Paris); Hedgehog bearing vessel, clay, Cyclades islands, Greece, c. 2300-2100 BC, National Archeological Museum, Athens (Edimedia, Paris). **144, 145:** Vase, ceramic with diorite, Egyptian, c. 3200-2800 BC (J. Guillot from C.d.S., Edimedia); Mixing bowl with flower decorations, ceramic, Minoan, c. 1850-1700 BC, Herakleion Museum, Crete (Ekdotike Athenon, Athens); Basket-shaped vase, stone, Minoan, c. 1700-1450 BC, Herakleion Museum, Crete (Ekdotike Athenon, Athens); Boot-shaped vessel, ceramic, Anatolian, c. 1800-1500 BC, The Metropolitan Museum of Art, Rogers Fund, 1967 (67.182.2). **148:** Palace of Erlitou, China, art by Greg Harlin of Stansbury, Ronsaville, Wood Inc., based on reconstruction by K. C. Chang. **151:** Detail, necklace, gold, Egyptian, Eighteenth Dynasty, c. 1550-1529 BC, Egyptian National Museum, Cairo (John G. Ross, Rome). **152, 153:** Battle-ax, copper and silver, Egyptian, c. 1800 BC, Trustees of the British Museum, London, EA 36776 — Spearhead, bronze, Minoan, c. 1450 BC, Ashmolean Museum, Oxford, AE 492 (Gordon Roberton) — Ax, bronze, Egyptian, c. 1900 BC, Trustees of the British Museum, London, EA 30083 — Knife, bronze, Egyptian, c. 1475 BC, Trustees of the British Museum, London, EA 6052 — Map of copper and tin sources by R. R. Donnelley & Sons Co., Cartographic Services; Fishhook, bronze, Sumerian, c. 2500 BC, Trustees of the British Museum, London, WA 120805. **154:** Animal finial, bronze, Anatolian, c. 2300-2100 BC, Anatolian Civilization Museum, Ankara (Ara Güler, Istanbul); Mirror, bronze, Egyptian, c. 1900 BC, Trustees of the British Museum, London, EA 37175. **155:** Skillet, bronze, Minoan, c. 1500-1450 BC, Ashmolean Museum, Oxford, 1967.1215 (Michael Freeman) — Razor, copper, Egyptian, c. 1900 BC, Trustees of the British Museum, London, EA 30070; Model of altar, copper, Egyptian, c. 2300 BC, Trustees of the British Museum, London, EA 5315 (Michael Holford, Loughton, Essex). **156:** Ax, silver with gold leaf, northern Afghanistan, c. 1900-1750 BC, The Metropolitan Museum of Art, Purchase, Harris Brisbane Dick Fund and James N. Spear and Schim-

mel Foundation Inc. Gifts, 1982 (1982.5); Vessel, silver, Sumerian, c. 3000 BC, Musée du Louvre/Réunion des Musées Nationaux, Paris. **157:** Map of silver sources by R. R. Donnelley & Sons Co., Cartographic Services — Kneeling bull holding vessel, silver, Elamite, c. 2900 BC, The Metropolitan Museum of Art, Purchase, Joseph Pulitzer Bequest, 1966 (66.173). **158,** 159: Map of gold sources by R. R. Donnelley & Sons Co., Cartographic Services; Helmet, gold, Sumerian, c. 2450 BC, Iraq Museum, Baghdad (Scala, Florence) — Dagger, gold, Sumerian, c. 2680-2520 BC, National Museum, Baghdad (Claus Hansmann, Stockdorf). **160:** Head of Horus, wood and bronze with gold plate, Egyptian, Sixth Dynasty, c. 2350 BC, Egyptian National Museum, Cairo (John G. Ross, Rome); Ewer, gold, Anatolian, c. 2100 BC, The Metropolitan Museum of Art, Harris Brisbane Dick Fund, 1957 (57.67). **161:** Cup, gold, Sumerian, c. 2500 BC, Trustees of the British Museum, London, WA 121346 — Human-headed bison, steatite and wood with gold overlay, Syrian, c. 2645-2415 BC, National Museum, Aleppo (Claus Hansmann, Stockdorf). **162:** Pendant, *The Master of Animals,* gold, Aegina, Greece, c. 1700-1500 BC, Trustees of the British Museum, London, GR 1892.5-20.8-cat. jewelry 762 — Bull's-head earring, gold, Minoan, c. 1700-1450 BC (Mike Dixon from Photoresources, Canterbury, Kent) — Necklace, gold, Aegina, Greece, c. 1700-1500 BC, Trustees of the British Museum, London, GR 1892.5-20.7-cat. jewelry 761. **163:** Necklace with fly pendants, gold, Egyptian, Eighteenth Dynasty, c. 1550-1529 BC, Egyptian National Museum, Cairo (John G. Ross, Rome) — Pendant, gold, Harappan, National Museum, New Delhi (Scala, Florence) — Necklace with pendants, gold, Mesopotamian, c. 1900-1800 BC, The Metropolitan Museum of Art, Fletcher Fund, 1947 (47.la-n). **164, 165:** Map of lapis lazuli and carnelian sources by R. R. Donnelley & Sons Co., Cartographic Services; Necklace with leaf pendants, gold, lapis lazuli, and carnelian, Sumerian, c. 2500 BC, Trustees of the British Museum, London, WA 1928.10-10,167; Necklace, carnelian and lapis lazuli, Mesopotamian, c. 2400 BC, Ashmolean Museum, Oxford, 1930-221 (Gordon Roberton) — Cowrie belt, gold, carnelian, and green feldspar, Egyptian, Twelfth Dynasty, 1994-1781 BC, The Metropolitan Museum of Art, contribution from Henry Walters and the Rogers Fund, 1916 (16.1.5) — Collar, gold and lapis lazuli, Sumerian, c. 2500 BC, Ashmolean Museum, Oxford, 1925-261 (Gordon Roberton).